PRAISE FOR

BANNON

"Darth Vader of the Right, populist Svengali, the real president, Stephen K. Bannon has been called many names, most counterfactual.

"I have worked with Steve inside and outside the White House. He is more than a Renaissance man. He is one of the truly strategic thinkers alive today. Keith Koffler's book will help you understand why Steve Bannon still matters, and why he is one of the most powerful and important men outside the Oval Office."

> **—SEBASTIAN GORKA, Ph.D.**, former deputy assistant to President Trump and chief strategist of the Make America Great Again Coalition

"By now, everyone in America knows Steve Bannon, the force of nature who has shaped the Trump presidency more than anyone except Trump himself. If you want to know what's behind that force of nature—if you want to know Steve Bannon the man—this is the indispensable book for you."

> **—DAVID HOROWITZ**, founding president of the David Horowitz Freedom Center and author of *Radical Son: A Generational Odyssey* and *Unholy Alliance: Radical Islam and the American Left*

"At a time when we are witnessing the wholesale abandonment of the basic principles of quality journalism—fairness, honesty, objective factual reportage, thoughtful analysis—all across the American media, it is most heartening to see Keith Koffler's *Bannon: Always the Rebel*. Mr. Koffler's treatment of his ostensibly controversial subject is at once dispassionate, informative, objective, and insightful. He more than meets his objectives of demystifying this important and not well-understood figure, placing Bannon accurately in the broader framework of American conservatism. The book is also a very lively read."

    —KENNETH deGRAFFENREID, former national security advisor to President Ronald Reagan and deputy undersecretary of defense

Bannon

BANNON

ALWAYS
THE REBEL

KEITH
KOFFLER

REGNERY
PUBLISHING
A Division of Salem Media Group

Regnery® is a registered trademark of Salem Communications Holding Corporation

Cataloging-in-Publication data on file with the Library of Congress

ISBN 978-1-62157-703-4
e-book ISBN 978-1-62157-737-9

Published in the United States by
Regnery Publishing
A Division of Salem Media Group
300 New Jersey Ave NW
Washington, DC 20001
www.Regnery.com

Manufactured in the United States of America

10 9 8 7 6 5 4 3 2 1

Books are available in quantity for promotional or premium use. For information on discounts and terms, please visit our website: www.Regnery.com.

For Rebekah, Adam, and Ariela

CONTENTS

INTRODUCTION   1

PROLOGUE   5

1 A BORN FIGHTER   9

2 THE CANDIDATE   19

3 IN THE NAVY   27

4 MOVING ON UP   35

5 THE AUTEUR   47

6 GENERATION ZERO   57

7 A FLAWED VISIONARY   69

8 STONE COLD SPIRITUAL   75

9 A HUMANE ECONOMY   83

10 DEFENDING THE WEST   103

11 TEA PARTY WARRIOR   117

12 THE PALIN PATRIOT   125

13 BANNON AT BREITBART   133

14 CAMPAIGN CHIEF   147

15 THE PRESIDENT'S STRATEGIST   165

EPILOGUE   185

ACKNOWLEDGMENTS   189

NOTES   191

INDEX   207

I am obliged to confess I should sooner live in a society governed by the first two thousand names in the Boston telephone directory than in a society governed by the two thousand faculty members of Harvard University.

—William F. Buckley Jr.

Introduction

This book is an effort to demystify Stephen Bannon, to separate the real man from the caricatures, and to explain his brand of conservative populism.

Bannon has a good sense of humor, but he is an extremely serious man. This I learned during more than ten hours of interviews with him, conducted over three different visits to his home in Washington, D.C. Two of the sessions occurred in July 2017, while he was in the White House serving as President Trump's chief strategist, and the other in August, just two days after his White House service ended. He is an impressive man to interview, a man whose mind is immersed not just in current events, but in history and philosophy and religion. "I don't think there is a major battle the United States has ever engaged in that Steve couldn't describe in minute detail," said one of his good friends. Indeed, during our conversations, generals and battles, world leaders and historical events, philosophers and theologians—from ancient times through the twenty-first century—dropped off Bannon's tongue with the ease of a blackjack dealer throwing cards on a table. If you find yourself facing off against him on *Jeopardy!* just quit or pray for the Daily Double.

Bannon is not only fearsomely learned, and always reading to learn more, he is committed to applying his knowledge to the world around him. Combine that with an incredible energy and will-power, little need for sleep, and a capacity for ruthlessness, and you have a force to be reckoned with or, for his enemies, preferably avoided.

Bannon is a rebel by nature, but always a rebel with a cause. That cause today is America, American culture, and the survival and prosperity of the American working and middle class. But as his sister Mary Beth told me, "He always had a purpose or something he was trying to fight for."[1]

Central to Bannon's thinking about America is his thinking about Western civilization, its Judeo-Christian tradition, and his own Catholic faith. "Bannon is a deeply faithful Catholic," one of his friends told me, and when I asked Bannon to provide me a shortlist of the books that have most influenced him, he gave me six, and I was surprised to see that three of them had to do with Christianity. The books were *The Imitation of Christ*, by Thomas à Kempis, *The Spiritual Exercises of St. Ignatius of Loyola*, *The Brotherhood of the Common Life and Its Influence*, by Ross Fuller, *The History of the Peloponnesian War*, by Thucydides, *The History of the Decline and Fall of the Roman Empire*, by Edward Gibbon, and *Lives of the Noble Greeks and Romans*, by Plutarch.

Western civilization today is under siege, in Bannon's view, from within and without. Many in the West have forgotten their culture or actively chosen to despise it; and he believes the West faces implacable enemies overseas, both Islamists and the Communist Chinese, who believe they can become the next great hegemonic power. The result of Bannon's thinking about how best to protect and defend America, its culture, and its Western tradition, at a time when its elites are manifestly corrupt, is a new conservative populism grounded in an old American economic system, known to historians as "The American System" or "Hamiltonian economics." Unlike most intellectuals—and indeed unlike many of the conservative intellectuals who run magazines and enjoy endowed chairs at think tanks—Bannon's ideas have actually translated into real politics. Indeed, no thinker was more important in helping to shape the pro-Trump populist rebellion than Steve Bannon; and no website was more influential in that endeavor than Breitbart.com, which Bannon leads, and which attracts tens of millions of readers.

One note on sourcing. When it was needed for the sake of clarity, I attached a footnote to comments Bannon and others made to me during interviews. But often I did not, so any quoted remarks that are not footnoted can be assumed to have been made to me.

This, then, is Bannon's story in brief; it is a guide to his principles and ideas, and perhaps a snapshot of America's future if Bannon's populist conservative movement succeeds.

Keith Koffler
August 25, 2017

The Rebel

The crowds lingered on the Washington Mall, but the Washington political establishment had already drifted back into the Capitol, still in disbelief about the dreadful scene it had just witnessed.

Almost no one among the Washington elite, Republican or Democrat, had wanted Donald J. Trump to be president of the United States. They thought he was unworthy of the office, a lout, an ignorant outsider.

Barack Obama, regardless of what one thought of his specific policies, was regarded by the political elites as a social and intellectual equal, a card-carrying member of the ruling class, an upholder of the liberal world order to which both political parties adhered.

Trump's election had shocked them; so had his Inaugural Address. Their view of the future was internationalist, based on global agreements and trade. They placed their faith in a prosperity driven by high technology and higher education. Most were liberal on immigration, on multiculturalism, and on social issues. They spoke for the class that took this as an orthodoxy that was beyond questioning or doubt.

But Trump spoke for all those millions of people who were not prospering, who saw their jobs being exported overseas, who saw their neighborhoods being surrendered to crime and illegal immigration, and, most important of all, who saw their America—its culture, history, and traditions—held in contempt by the political and media elite. They saw the America they knew and loved being lost; they foresaw a future of socialism, of official hostility to religion and traditional values, of a balkanized country where the Democrats used identity politics for electoral gain; they feared the American Dream might not exist for their children if Hillary Clinton were elected.

Unlike the elite, Trump understood these fears, believed they were well-founded, and wanted, apparently sincerely, to take action on behalf of the common American, to "make," as he said, "America great again." To return power to the people.

"Today," Trump announced, "we are not merely transferring power from one Administration to another, or from one party to another—but we are transferring power from Washington, D.C. and giving it back to you, the American people. For too long, a small group in our nation's capital has reaped the rewards of government while the people have borne the cost. Washington flourished—but the people did not share in its wealth. Politicians prospered—but the jobs left, and the factories closed. The establishment protected itself, but not the citizens of our country. Their victories have not been your victories; their triumphs have not been your triumphs; and while they celebrated in our nation's capital, there was little to celebrate for struggling families all across our land."

"January 20th, 2017, will be remembered as the day the people became the rulers of this nation again," Trump declared. "The forgotten men and women of our country will be forgotten no longer."[1]

As the shell-shocked political elite stumbled back to their chambers, or headed home to change into evening dress for the obligatory inaugural balls or merely to pour themselves a stiff drink and watch the events on television, two of Trump's closest aides weren't ready to depart. They strode down to the railing at the front of the platform from which the president had spoken.

Stephen Miller was a thirty-one-year-old conservative populist firebrand. He had worked for conservative Republican Senator Jeff Sessions—the first U.S. senator to support Trump, and now slated to become attorney general—before joining Trump campaign as a speechwriter. With Miller was Stephen Bannon, a political neophyte who had become the chief executive officer of Trump's campaign. Bannon, a brilliant and deeply knowledgeable man, was an ideological soulmate of Trump, and he helped guide the campaign along the populist-nationalist script Trump had conceived.

Miller and Bannon had been up all night helping the president-elect in any way they could, even down to making sure the teleprompter would roll in the drizzling rain that was expected on Inauguration Day. Weary but still fueled by a fading dose of adrenaline, they looked out over the Mall, from the Capitol out toward the Washington Monument. Trump had practiced the speech endlessly, and as far as Miller and Bannon were concerned, he had risen to the moment and crushed it.

"You know, it was just perfect," Miller said of Trump's delivery of his speech. "Just perfect."

Bannon thought for a moment. "There's only one problem," he said.

"What's that?" wondered Miller.

"The only mistake we made is we had the podium pointed the wrong way. We should have turned the podium around and had it face the group of swells on the platform."

The Trump Revolution had begun—and Bannon was Trump's rebel-in-chief.

CHAPTER ONE

A Born Fighter

To understand Stephen Bannon, you need to understand that he was a working-class Irish-Catholic kid from Richmond, Virginia, whose family voted Democrat, supported civil rights, and were patriotic. The values he learned as a child—to favor the underdog and the working man, to love your country, your family, and your faith—stuck with him.

Nevertheless, he was a born rebel and fighter: headstrong, independent, pugnacious, stubborn, willful, insisting on walking to kindergarten himself (not holding his mother's hand), splashing in puddles (when that was forbidden because it would ruin his only pair of shoes), and unafraid to take on older kids at the basketball court (with his fists if not with the ball).

Stephen Kevin Bannon was born in Norfolk, Virginia, on November 27, 1953, with an older sister, Sharon, an older brother,

Martin "Mike" Bannon III, and, in due course, a younger brother, Chris, and sister, Mary Beth.

By the time Stephen was five, the Bannon family had moved into the modest, middle-class home in the Ginter Park section of Richmond where his father, Martin Bannon Sr., has lived ever since. There was no dishwasher, no dryer, and in sweltering, humid Richmond, no air conditioning. "It was a very simple life," said Sharon. "We didn't have frills but we didn't know we didn't," said Chris. "I think maybe once or twice a year our parents would take us out to dinner somewhere, really as an etiquette lesson almost as much as a celebration of a report card or something."

While they lived in Ginter Park, their other "neighborhood" was the Catholic parishes of a mostly Protestant city. Richmond's Catholics were a "very tight community," said Pat McSweeney, a close family friend who was Mike Bannon's age. Richmond's Catholics knew each other, sent their children to the same Catholic schools, and were serious about their religion. This meant raising kids by the Golden Rule, with an emphasis on values and proper behavior, church attendance on Sunday, and prayers seven days a week. The Bannon family attended church in their Sunday best—young Stephen was an altar boy—and celebrated every Sunday with a grand family dinner.

It was a very "traditional Catholic upbringing," said McSweeney, and "It was pretty thoroughgoing. It was not something that was confined to Sunday or to school. It infused everything." The community was so tight that "We were not only disciplined by our parents, but the parents of our friends."[1]

*

As a young man, Steve Bannon's father had been a superb athlete. When he was eighteen, the Washington Senators drafted him as a catcher for one of their farm teams. He was promised a baseball bat and a salary of $50 a month. "I signed the contract and I was assigned to a team in the Appalachian League—out in Tennessee—and I did not report," said Bannon in July 2017, still sharp and brimming with humor at the age of ninety-five.

C&P Telephone of Virginia, where he was already working, paid better and seemed to offer a more solid future. "To start off in 1939 I made $16 a week," he said. "Social Security had just started and they took 16 cents out of my pay, so I got $15.84. In 1939 that was one of the best paying jobs in town when you first got on to work. And it had some benefits and some security."[2]

The Senators weren't done with him, though. They upped their offer to $75 a month. But Martin still didn't show up. "He was a holdout!" cracked his son Mike Bannon, who shares his father's mischievous sense of humor.[3] The Senators eventually sent Martin a notice that he had been "suspended" for failing to report, and that was the end of Martin's brief inning as a professional baseball player.

At C&P, which was part of the AT&T network, Martin began in Norfolk, Virginia, as a cable splicer's "helper." In his early years, he could be found on the outskirts of town clambering up telephone poles to work on wires dozens of feet above the ground—or down in the sewers, where wire was often laid closer to the center of the city. By 1955, he was a manager in Richmond, where he would stay and steadily gain greater and greater responsibility.

In 1942, he married Doris Virginia Anita Herr—originally of Baltimore, Maryland—in Norfolk, Virginia. They were both twenty years old.

Where Martin was reserved, somewhat cautious, and practical, Doris was by all accounts a vivacious dreamer and charmer, a woman who dominated every room she entered, a "force of nature," were the words used by several of her friends. "She never drove, she didn't have a car, and yet she was everywhere," said her eldest daughter, Sharon. "We'd say she was the original Uber because she found people to take her places."

She talked a lot. "It was hard to get a word in," McSweeney wryly noted. But she listened too, and she probed. "She was a very interesting woman, and was always interested in whatever we were doing," McSweeney said, from jobs to college majors.[4]

"She'd want to get to know you. She'd want to hear everything about you," said Sharon. "And her big thing was jobs. "We called her the Patron Saint of Jobs because if she met you and you didn't have a job, she would go and find a job for you, and she'd call you up and say, 'I got an interview for you at this place. You tell them that I sent you.'"[5]

"She was very, very warm, very approachable," remembered Scot Vorse, who met Steve Bannon at Harvard Business School and later became his business partner. "Strong-willed, good quality person, very strong personality. She was a spitfire, man."[6]

She eventually became the coolest grandma around, leaping off diving boards and going on roller coasters, so it was a shock to the entire family when she died suddenly of a massive stroke in January 1992 at the age of sixty-nine. Martin Bannon had just retired and had been planning for the couple's fiftieth wedding anniversary.

Aside from her vivacity, Doris had another characteristic that stood out in Richmond in the 1940s, '50s, and '60s. She was a liberal, opposed to segregation, and vocal about it.

The Bannons were also wild about Jack Kennedy, more so than most Richmond Catholics, according to McSweeney, because the Bannons "were a little more liberal than most of the folks in that circle," who had their doubts about the Kennedys' fidelity to the faith.

Steve Bannon adopted his mother's liberalism and maintained it through his college years, though like his mother, his outlook was always informed by the basic conservatism of a strict Catholic upbringing. From his father, Bannon learned discipline, hard work, and practicality. From his mother, he inherited an indomitable personality and intensity, a whirlwind conversational style, a keen interest in others, and a desire to help the underdog. And, like her, he was a dreamer.

The dreamer in Bannon expressed itself in at least two ways: his varied future career and the deep intellectual architecture that would eventually undergird his political beliefs. "Steve can't do something forever and ever," his sister Mary Beth said, mentioning his transition from being a Navy officer to working on Wall Street, and a career that eventually took him from Hollywood, to journalism, to politics and the White House.[7]

But along with a restless spirit, there were certain constants. The Bannon children had a sense of morality and patriotism drilled into them by their pious and patriotic parents. Martin Bannon says he taught his kids "cheerfulness, loyalty, and to be God-fearing," as well as modesty. "Dad always said a good product doesn't need advertising," said Sharon. "We were just supposed to do what was right whether anybody was watching or not," said Mary Beth.

They were also taught to be industrious. Once they became teenagers, the Bannon children were expected to work over their summer vacations. One summer, Steve took a job in a junkyard, where he got so dirty that his mother hosed him off every night when he came home. "He doesn't like the easy jobs," said Mary Beth. "He likes to challenge himself, that's the big thing about

Steve." But he also learned he wanted to be successful, because he didn't want his future to lie in a junkyard.

A hard worker himself, Bannon was deeply impressed by the work ethic of an African American man named Nat James, who jogged to work because he didn't have a car. "This guy I work with, he's the hardest working human being I've ever seen," Steve told the family at the dinner table. "He does the job of three men." Steve introduced Nat to his father, who was impressed and got him a night job working for the phone company, which he did in addition to his job at the junkyard.

Another summer, Steve took a factory job with Bethlehem Steel, working the swing shift from three p.m. to eleven p.m. After a few weeks, those working the shift were laid off. The factory manager promised it was just a temporary thing and they'd soon be back on the job. Steve believed it, but Doris didn't. When Doris extracted the truth from the manager, that those jobs were gone, Bannon was appalled, thinking of his colleagues who had families to support and who were now out of a job. "I think it had an impact on him," his brother Chris said. Steve saw "these great people, these hard-working people, and they lied to them."

★

"He's highly competitive," said Chris of his brother Steve. "He was never the greatest athlete, but he'd figure ways to compete and win. He doesn't like to lose."

Doing what it took to win caused problems at the nearby Ginter Park Community Center, where Steve swam, played basketball, shot pool, and occasionally got into fights.

"Steve was—to say 'aggressive' is probably mild," McSweeney said. "He was not the most talented basketball player, but the most aggressive. It was a reputation that preceded him."

Tough kids, older than Steve, would hang out near the community center, smoking cigarettes and looking for a fight. Bannon was always happy to give them one. "Steve's not a guy to take a lot of guff....He's not going to get pushed around," said Chris.

"Back then in a basketball game you called your own fouls.... Steve would call a foul and maybe one of the other guys disagreed with that, and Steve was not so diplomatic, and the next thing you know," it was on. "He was a brawler from an early age. If he thinks he's right, he's not backing off."

Steve seemed to relish combat. Even when he lost a fight and his brother Mike had to bring him home, he'd slip out the door as soon as he could to take his opponents on again. His brother Mike recounted, "I said I don't mind you fighting all these guys but could you make it a little less than eight?"[8]

Sometimes the battles were internecine. "Steve's the kind of guy—he knows your pressure points—he knows everybody's pressure points—and he knows when to push them," said Chris. "And my older brother and him, they'd go. It wasn't unusual to see Mike and Steve rolling down the steps from the second floor."

Oddly, while he was a brawler, he was a bookish brawler, and from a young age. By the time he was nine or ten, he was already a voracious reader of the classics of Western literature. He slept little and read much—a habit that he maintains to this day. He was always an autodidact eager to improve his mind and learn more. As he got older, this led him to take a speed-reading course at Georgetown and sign up for Toastmasters to improve his public speaking. "He was always looking to improve himself, make himself more competitive, give himself more tools in his belt," Chris said. "He had no qualms about going out and using whatever was out there to do that."[9]

Steve once got angry with his younger brother Chris for reading comic books when he thought he should be reading serious books. "He ordered books and they come to the house and he'd grab that box and run upstairs and open it and just sort through them and grab one and get up on his bed and start reading it," said Chris. His sister Mary Beth says that even now, when Steve comes to Richmond to visit, he heads into used bookstores and emerges with piles of books. "All his houses today, they have beds in them, but they're libraries," said Chris. "He buys houses to store all his books in. He goes in and builds bookshelves and puts books on them."

The family describes a child who was always goal-oriented. Mary Beth remembered "He had like, a list—I'm gonna do this, and then I'm gonna do this," which included, interestingly enough, working at the White House.

His dreams of future success were backed not just by a strong work ethic but by a crafty entrepreneurial streak. "At 12 years old when he has a paper route, he realizes, hey I've got a 'client base,'" said Chris. "I think dad takes him down to the farmers' market in downtown Richmond and all the farmers bring their stuff on the weekends, and we'd get some fresh vegetables and bring them home. Well, Steve sees that, puts two and two together, he takes his paperboy money, buys fruits and vegetables, brings them home, and then takes them around to all his 'clients' and sells them vegetables and produce and makes money on it."

Like many other boys of that time, Steve and Chris loved analyzing the player statistics on baseball cards, but Steve's love of statistics and data carried over into the stock market as well.

Chris remembered that while he would read the sports page and the comics in the newspaper, "Steve would read the sports page, the comics, and the stock page." Steve would "pick stocks and write them in a notebook and…watch what they did."

★

In 1968, Steve, like his brother Mike before him, was sent to an all-male Catholic military academy, Benedictine High School. Many Catholic children in Richmond went either to Benedictine or to its sister school, St. Gertrude's. There was plenty of discipline and order to be found at both. At Benedictine, if the monks didn't hand it out to you, the military teachers would. "There was a great deal of discipline there. We had to shine our shoes, polish our brass, keep your hair cut close," said McSweeney, who also attended the school. "We had an honor system, and we behaved according to a model or a standard that was established by the commandant and the faculty." The kids carried around Korean War–issue M14s, minus the firing pin. "We had a whole arsenal," said Chris, who attended the school with Steve.

The place was an oasis of tradition and regimen in an America that was starting to be torn apart by the leftist protest movements of the late 1960s. "We had to take Latin and logic—everyone had to take a classical education program—and a heavy dose of values," said McSweeney. "At that time, most of the teachers were monks. It was very definitely a religious education."[10]

Bannon made the honor roll his freshman year, but never again. According to Chris, he was a "solid A or B" student with maybe a few C's thrown in. He was a class secretary his sophomore year, on the debate team his sophomore and junior years, and was an "officer" at the school, but only as a second lieutenant. In his senior year he served as a "defense counsel" on the military court.

Chris suggested Bannon's relative lack of "distinction" had much to do with his rebelliousness, individualism, and consequent lack of interest in officially sanctioned honors. Nevertheless, the other students looked up to him, even if he didn't have a formal leadership role. "You got two types of leaders in all walks of life: you got the goody two shoes, the guys who at our school were called 'licks,' which meant bootlickers," Chris said. "And Steve is kind of always the fly in the ointment a little bit. Even then he was the anti-establishment guy. He's the guy fighting the system. They had a military court in the school for your demerits and stuff, Steve's a defense guy. He's defending the guys." No doubt, some of the alleged offenders were his friends. He tended to hang out with "the rowdier guys," Chris said.

But while Bannon would challenge the system, he wasn't the kind to drop out of it. "When he has to be, he's towing the line for the good of the school, but other times he's constantly challenging it," Chris said. "Steve was a guy who was in the system, did have success, but was always challenging."[11] Late in high school, he started bearing down on his studies, his competitive drive kicking in to get him into a good college; that college would be Virginia Tech.

CHAPTER TWO

The Candidate

Bannon said he chose Virginia Tech because he was a fan of Hokie football and many of his friends, especially Benedictine kids, went to Virginia Tech. Bannon reminisced that "when you're up at Tech, it feels like almost home."[1]

Virginia Tech was especially strong as an engineering school, but engineering wasn't for him. "They have a course that starts the first day for engineers. It's called 'Five Hour Calculus,'" Bannon said. The purpose of the early morning, hour-long, five-day course "is to weed out guys who want to be real engineers from the guys who just want to pretend to be engineers. They literally went through all the math I knew in two days."[2]

As for his other options, Bannon recalled, "I had no interest in business at all. I realized my dad would never let me be a history or philosophy major. So I looked around. When I had to declare a major, the college of architecture had all the cool kids, all the kids from up north, all the hot girls, all the artistes, all the girls wearing berets." After four years in a Catholic military academy, he felt he was ready for something different, but "I also realized," he confessed, "I'm not an architect. But they had a major in the college of architecture that was a grab bag. It was called environmental and urban studies." That sounded good enough—it kept him in the college of architecture.[3]

Friends from his college days remember Bannon as smart, studious, popular, and a leader. Academically, according to his dad, he started out poorly his freshman year but picked up steam and was eventually scoring A's. In 1975, when he ran to become student government president, he won convincingly. "He was very approachable and very engaging," said Mark Krivoruchka, a classmate who worked on Bannon's campaign for student president. "He was popular."[4]

He was also something of a ladies' man. "I remember he had very attractive young ladies around him all the time," said Mike McLaughlin, who opposed Bannon for student government president.[5] According to Peter Alberice, Bannon's junior and senior year roommate, and perhaps his closest friend on campus—the two still keep in touch—Bannon had four steady girlfriends during his time at Virginia Tech. The fourth, Cathleen "Susie" Houff, whom he dated his senior year, would go on to become his first wife and the mother of his first child, Maureen Bannon. Alberice said he didn't think Bannon was especially profligate. "That depends on who you ask," Alberice said when asked if Bannon was a ladies' man. "To me, a ladies' man is someone who was going out with someone different every month. And that wasn't him."[6]

It might be surprising, given Bannon's current image—one of dishevelment and five o'clock shadow—but at the time, many people thought he looked a bit like a wavy-haired Robert Redford.

"He's a handsome guy," said Susan Oliver, a friend, but not a girl-friend, of Bannon, who ran successfully as his vice president for student body leadership.[7] Indeed, Bannon appeared in a photo with Oliver in the August 1975 edition of *Glamour* magazine. She, Bannon, and some other Virginia Tech students were profiled for their work in helping to make it a crime to sell pre-written term papers in Virginia. "He looks like Joe cool in the picture," she said.[8] In the photo, Bannon is thin, preppily garbed in white khakis, a pale blue polo shirt, and a casual brown sports jacket. His dad ribbed him about the photo shoot: "I have two daughters, and my son has to be in *Glamour* magazine."

Darrell Nevin, who also roomed with Bannon, was less impressed. He remembers a young man who was a heavy drinker and whose relationships with women often ended in tears. "I wouldn't say there were dozens of situations like that, but that was the memory of how they ended. They ended badly, let's put it that way. He was fawned over by the women, and sometimes took advantage of that."[9]

Oliver, his running mate in the contest for student body president, was much more positive. "He does not have a sexist, racist bone in his body. I don't even remember a single solitary inappropriate word that he used, let alone any action," said Oliver. "When Steve decided to run for president, back then, 42 years ago, it was a big deal for him to ask me, as a woman, to be his running mate," she said. "Women didn't run for things like that back then. I was very grateful." And once in office, he delegated to her. "He allowed me to do my job and he wanted me to be successful."

Steve's brother Mike suggested an additional reason for putting Oliver on the ticket: voter demographics. The number of women at Virginia Tech had grown rapidly in the decade before Bannon arrived in 1972 from about three hundred to four thousand.[10]

"Steve came in and ran with a brilliant strategy—he ran with a woman," said Mike.[11]

Oliver thought that Bannon, even then, was "extraordinarily brilliant" and had a "laser focus."[12]

"You know, there's the look that he has, that really intense look? He had that back in school," Alberice said. "I mean he could zero in on something and he would be so focused on it." That was especially true of his reading, which was wide, intense, and eclectic, though he especially loved reading history, and he loved big ideas. "He was interested in everything. He was definitely interested in how things related to each other."[13] He was, by all accounts, among the more intellectual of his peers, but he was also down to earth.

According to Oliver, Bannon "was very conscientious, very hard working, very dedicated." As students, she said, "We took the world we were in seriously. We're not these little kids running around college grinning from ear to ear like kids are today." Bannon was even nominated by a professor for a Rhodes Scholarship. According to Oliver, Bannon qualified based on academic and leadership credentials but lacked a varsity letter that was needed at the time.[14] Not that he was unathletic. Friends marveled at his ability to scale rock formations down by the New River just outside of Blacksburg, and he was a good intramural football player, just as later, in the Navy, he was regarded as an aggressive, if single-minded, basketball player (nicknamed, not entirely affectionately, "Coast" as in "coast to coast" for his habit of taking the ball at one end of the court and racing down to shoot it at the other; passing the ball never crossed his mind). But without a jacket with the letters "VT" sewn into it, there was no Rhodes Scholarship.

Bannon then, as now, was something of an activist, and, according to Oliver and Alberice, a liberal. "Very liberal," said

Alberice, though an "old school" Democrat, focused more on economic issues that would benefit the working class. Neither Bannon nor Oliver was interested in the extreme protest antics of the 1960s and 1970s; in fact, Bannon would regard them as irresponsible and self-indulgent. As Oliver recollected, he was low-key, and "I don't ever remember anything being about Steve personally. He was never trying to promote himself. Steve was never about promoting Steve." Oliver says she and Bannon weren't "rabble rousers," but rather felt a responsibility to the students, who they believed deserved a greater voice in university decisions. "He was genuinely concerned about the direction the university was going in, in the same way he's genuinely concerned today about where Western Civilization is going," Oliver said. "He's doing now exactly what he was doing then in trying to be a positive force for the changes that need to be made. He's not out there rioting in the street and burning cars and all that kind of whatever. He didn't do that then and he's not doing that now." They disdained those sorts of protest as a waste of time.[15]

Nevertheless, Bannon's strong beliefs did sometimes lead to unusual undertakings. "One time my parents came up and made a reservation at a nice restaurant and he was like, 'I can't come because I'm protesting something and I'm on a starvation diet,'" said his sister Mary Beth. At another point, Bannon apparently got it into his head that he needed to be closer to nature. "I know at Virginia Tech he wanted to live in a tent one year, and my parents were very upset," Mary Beth said. "They were like, 'No, you're not going to live in a tent.'" So instead, he moved into an old farmhouse that had no electricity.

Perhaps surprisingly, Bannon also opposed the Vietnam War, as did Oliver, who was a delegate to the 1972 Democratic convention that nominated the very liberal, anti-war George McGovern for president. Bannon's opposition to the Vietnam War actually predated his enrollment at Virginia Tech. Bannon was not a radical leftist who thought America was evil and Ho Chi Minh was a Communist saint, but he did think the war was not in America's national interest. According to his brother, Mike, Bannon disapproved of the way the war was being fought and was skeptical about what we would now call "nation-building" abroad. At a military academy like Benedictine, "that didn't go over too well," his dad noted.[16]

Bannon, who had only joined the Virginia Tech student government his junior year, was running for president against what was effectively the establishment. One of his opponents was Marshall DeBerry, who'd spent more time in the trenches and was the choice of the outgoing president. DeBerry was part of the old, "weak" order Bannon said he was campaigning against. "He was saying, 'This administration, these guys…they're all part of this old crowd. They haven't done jack for you," DeBerry recalled.[17]

"Don't be fooled by Bannon. He has immense charisma, but lacks the ability to keep his head geared in any one particular direction long enough to accomplish anything," wrote Gary Clisham, whom Bannon was running to replace, in a letter to the editor of the student newspaper.[18]

Bannon kept his head geared in a single direction long enough to win in a landslide. He received 2,676 votes, more than double the second-place finisher, Mike McLaughlin, who got only 1,080. DeBerry came in third with 688. The Bannon-Oliver administration was in. Mike Bannon described it as a "pivotal moment" for Steve. It showed he was "disruptor" with the leadership skills necessary to buck the establishment. And, like his then-hero John F. Kennedy, he had charisma. "He was very articulate and good looking," said McLaughlin.[19] "He had style points that other candidates did not," said Bannon's room-mate Darrell Nevin. "The previous folks were more buttoned down, straight arrows. And he represented more of, I call it the casual elite, if you will." He was just cooler than the competition, and "he played his card well," Nevin said.[20]

Oliver says that once in power the following year, the Bannon-Oliver administration was able to bring the students, and student concerns, into the dean's office when important decisions were being made. "We, through our administration, obtained seats at the table," she said. "Whenever any of those meetings took place, students were present as a result of the work that Steve and I did."[21]

Bannon was "a natural born leader" and could get things done, according to Alberice. "He was a great organizer."[22]

It surprised many of his fellow students when this most intel-lectual of their friends finished college in 1976 and joined the Navy. "I admired him for wanting to join the military," said Oliver, whose own father had served. Nevin, who thought Bannon needed more self-discipline in his life, had a different take. "I was like, well that will straighten his ass out."[23]

Bannon had been offered a job with Philip Morris, a major employer in Richmond, and a lock on a steady, lucrative career. It was hard for his family to understand why he would pass up such a golden opportunity for security. "To get a job with Philip Morris was big-time. It was hard to do back then," said his sister Sharon. But Bannon felt, as his sister Mary Beth related, that he just couldn't sit in an office at a nine-to-five job.[24] The Navy offered not just service, which was attractive to him, but adventure; and while Bannon's father was surprised at his son's career choice, he was also excited. He had been unable to join the military during World War II because of a minor medical issue, and he had always regret-ted that he hadn't served. Many in his deeply patriotic family had, and some of them were buried in Arlington Cemetery. He was proud of his son's choice.

That summer, Bannon parked cars to make some money. And in the fall, he entered Officer Candidate School.

CHAPTER THREE

In the Navy

Bannon served seven years with the United States Navy. He was repeatedly praised by senior officers and promoted from ensign to lieutenant junior grade to lieutenant. A portion of his service was aboard the USS *Paul F. Foster*, a destroyer assigned to protect aircraft carriers. One of its primary duties was tracking Soviet submarines.[1]

Aboard the *Foster*, Bannon, was "assigned to a windowless, two-bed stateroom with desks and a wardrobe area, a comfortable accommodation compared with the warren of bunks where most sailors slept. His first job gave him responsibility for engineering, including air conditioning, hydraulics, and electronics. Bannon later became a navigator, guiding the ship—at times with a sextant when the electronic system lost contact with satellites—and writing reports."[2]

Bannon served four years at sea and then three at the Pentagon as an aide to the chief of naval operations. He "was a very good problem solver," recalled one of his superiors. "When I had a problem that I needed help on, he was a good guy to go to. And he knew people in the Pentagon who knew the answers when I needed answers."[3] Bannon was part of the chief of naval operations executive board, "an ad hoc group to study something quickly," said retired Rear Admiral Sonny Masso, who was a close friend aboard the Foster and then at the Pentagon. The executive board "could get something fast and get the 65 or the 75 percent solution to the CNO." Then the CNO would decide what else needed to be done.

While in the Navy, according to several accounts, the studious, ambitious Bannon saw himself as a future secretary of defense, but Masso said that he never thought Bannon regarded the Navy as a career move: "He didn't have an agenda like, 'I'm here because it's going to help me later when I run for president.'"

Rather, Masso said it was a sense of duty instilled in Bannon by his father, Martin, and his years of schooling at Benedictine that encouraged his desire to serve in the Navy. "A lot of his core goes back to Martin Bannon," said Masso, remarking that the elder Bannon should be "canonized and become a servant of God and a Saint immediately after he passes away." Martin Bannon "is a guy that loved his country, worked hard, took care of his family, and there was that ethos in his family that, it was just understood that people are going to serve."

But even if the Navy was not a direct path to something else, it was a way station where Bannon learned important lessons that would help forge his character. Ironically, in the most hierarchical of organizations, Masso says he and Bannon were fortunate enough to come under the command during their time at sea of someone who inspired them to show initiative. "We were influenced by a guy named Captain George Sullivan," Masso said. "And George had a bias toward action, and he taught us this. Get it done, freakin' now. This doesn't mean cutting corners ethically, this means, if we are planning to train to do something, let's do it today and let's get it done now." This helped shape and confirm Bannon's own inclinations. "A guy like Steve, he brings this bias toward action," Masso said.

Masso thinks Sullivan's lessons relate directly to Bannon's impatience with government bureaucracy. Masso said that in Bannon's view, "When you hear people that want to be thoughtful, and pensive, and they want to deliberate, and they want an inquiry, and they want to look for second, and third, and fourth order effects—they want to think about all the unintended consequences that might arise. All those are words for the Deep State. That's code words for, 'we're going to be passive aggressive, we're not going to get anything done. Maybe we'll move something from the inbox to the outbox today.'"[4]

Other captains who took over after Sullivan were happy to have a pair of junior officers who could get things done. "These other captains fucking loved us," Masso said. "They were like 'Man, these guys are irreverent.' Nobody outworked us. Nobody outplayed us. Nobody out-decided us. We had our shit together. We walked with a spring in our step. And the other captains, they loved it. They loved the style." He added, "We worked and played hard."[5]

The *Foster* was initially part of the carrier group sent to the Persian Gulf in Jimmy Carter's abortive attempt to rescue the Americans held hostage by militant Iranian "students" who had seized the U.S. Embassy after an Islamist revolution had overthrown the Shah of Iran. The *Foster* departed from the Gulf of Oman for Pearl Harbor before the rescue mission, Operation Eagle Claw, was launched.

When Bannon and his crewmates found out about the tragic end to the aborted mission—which left eight crewmen dead and four injured when two of the rescue helicopters collided after Carter canceled the operation—they were deeply demoralized, and it affected Bannon's view of Carter.[6] But according to those who knew him at the time, it only accelerated or finalized Bannon's conversion from liberal to conservative, Democrat to Republican. He was in some ways a prototypical "Reagan Democrat," who thought the Democratic Party was no longer the party of the little guy, but an incompetent leftist outfit that was wrong on defense, wrong on social issues, and even wrong on the economy. Bannon family friend Pat McSweeney said that his and Bannon's views evolved somewhat in parallel during the late 1970s and early 1980s. "I know Steve began to feel the same impulse I did," said McSweeney, who eventually became chairman of the Republican Party in Virginia.[7] Both men came to loathe Jimmy Carter and venerate Ronald Reagan.

Under Jimmy Carter, the country seemed to be entering a period of rapid decline. As Bannon's Navy friend Sonny Masso noted, it wasn't just the failed rescue attempt or the fall of the Shah or Communist expansion overseas. Domestically, "It was just one thing after another," including gas lines, rising unemployment, and inflation. Bannon, who maintained his interest in stocks and statistics, kept a tally on the so-called misery index (a combination of unemployment and inflation) which skyrocketed under Carter to the highest level ever in postwar American history. The misery extended to the entire mood of the country, and maybe especially to the military, which had seemingly come in for nothing but criticism and contempt since the Vietnam War.

By the time of the presidential debate between Ronald Reagan and Jimmy Carter, Bannon was squarely in Reagan's corner. Masso recalled that Bannon, who watched the debate on television, "didn't sit. He watched that like a prize fight." At "every point," he felt "it was imperative" that Reagan score with a clean hit.[8] Bannon was elated after Reagan won the election.

When Reagan took office, military officers in Washington mostly wore civilian clothes. Soon after the new president was inaugurated, a story made its way around Washington that Reagan in his first weeks on the job had met with one of his top brass and wondered, "How do I know you're a general if you don't wear a uniform?" Before you knew it, military officials were once again snappily attired in uniform.[9] Bannon—then working at the Pentagon, and who himself had been wearing uniforms since high school, with a preppy interlude, of course, in college—ate it up. According to Masso, Carter had made military officials pay to park at the Pentagon. "Reagan said," not only am I going to end that policy, "but I'm going to refund whatever you did pay," Masso remembered. "This got our attention."

Reagan made rebuilding our military a priority, including plans to construct a six-hundred-ship Navy. By 1987, he had come just six ships short.[10]

He also made a point of reaffirming American patriotism and pride in our military. On February 24, 1981, the new president traveled to the Pentagon to award the Medal of Honor to Vietnam veteran Roy Benavidez. In the course of his remarks, Reagan said:

> Several years ago, we brought home a group of American fighting men who had obeyed their country's call and who had fought as bravely and as well as any Americans in our history. They came home without a victory not because they'd been defeated, but because they'd been denied permission to win. They were greeted by no

parades, no bands, no waving of the flag they had so
nobly served. There's been no 'thank you' for their sacrifice. There's been no effort to honor and, thus, give
pride to the families of more than 57,000 young men
who gave their lives in that faraway war.[11]

Masso and Bannon witnessed those remarks in person and
were deeply impressed. "Ronald Reagan called the Vietnam war
for the first time, a war that we were denied permission to win,"
Masso said. "That speech, in that moment, in that day, and all the
things that preceded it, created this aura that it was okay to be
patriotic."

Patriotism was something the Democratic Party had seemed to
leave behind as it became the party of the counterculture, of "Acid,
Amnesty [for draft dodgers], and Abortion," (in Robert Novak's
phrase covering the 1972 campaign), the party of "blame America
first" (as former Democrat and Reagan's ambassador to the United
Nations, Jeane Kirkpatrick, would call it), and the party of Cart-
eresque ineptitude.

Bannon's college roommate Peter Alberice remembers that "We
were kind of the same way, just old school Democrat—Truman/
Kennedy Democrats that were more about factory jobs and more
focused economically on the middle class and the lower middle
class and the lower class rather than worrying about peripheral
issues that the Democratic Party is stuck on right now."[12]

Bannon's Democrat background was important, because while
he became a conservative, he was never "Chamber of Commerce
Republican" or a libertarian free-market absolutist. His politics
were rooted in patriotism, nationalism, a concern for the common
man, and a defense of American culture and Western civilization.
He had seen a lot of the world as a Navy officer, and he knew that

America, and the West, represented a civilization worth defending. Of course, that civilization relied, in part, on a successful economy, and Bannon never neglected that fact. In the Navy, "He was the only 22 or 24-year-old I knew who subscribed to and read the *Wall Street Journal* cover to cover," Masso said. "He had a stock broker named Mr. Moody, and he was doing call and put options and looking at the price of silver and gold. It would inspire major conversation among the shipmates about matters that most 24-year-olds" don't care about.[13]

Bannon, when not in uniform, liked to play golf. He was a decent athlete. He liked to run, to work out. He was in great shape. "That's an irony, because now he looks like a slob," Masso said affectionately. "But he was a big preppy guy. He wore IZOD, Lacoste shirts, no socks with his penny loafers, pink shirts with khaki pants and blue sports coat."[14]

And he was still all about self-improvement, getting a master's degree in national security studies from Georgetown, working on it as a naval officer, and in 1985, two years after he left the Navy, earning an MBA from Harvard.[15]

That too would be a formative experience.

CHAPTER FOUR

Moving on Up

Bannon began at Harvard Business School in 1983. He was older than most of his classmates, a couple months shy of his thirtieth birthday. He already had seven years in the Navy under his belt, and he was married. He knew more than the others, and the military had given him a sense of command, and he soon showed it.

Around the beginning of the school year, in a class of about ninety people, Bannon seated himself in the "skydeck" overlooking the herd below. The professor peered up at the strategically situated student and asked him to present the case study the class had been assigned, something having to do with a bedding maker named Fieldcrest Blankets. "This," Bannon deadpanned, "is a sleepy industry."[1] Having cracked up the class, he proceeded to wow them by coolly hitting his presentation out of the park. "He put the fear of God into everybody because he was very impressive," said a fellow student, Scot Vorse.

Another student, Cornelia Tilney, recalled, "He was quite gutsy and pretty much blew the class away with an incredible performance. I remember thinking after watching him, 'I am definitely flunking this class if this is where the bar is set!'"[2]

Bannon became one of the most significant figures at a school filled with driven individuals. "Big personality, confident, aggressive, smart," was how Vorse described him.[3]

Vorse met Bannon at a student reception the day before school began. They hit it off pretty quickly, and Bannon, ever the organizer, asked Vorse to join his study group of about seven people. Vorse said, "He was an extremely hard worker. Very obsessive worker."

At first, Bannon took the lead in the relationship. "It really was initially a big brother little brother relationship," Vorse said. "You know, I was 22 and he was 29 at the time. We became very, very close friends." The sibling friendship was not without rivalry. "He and I came back across the Harvard Bridge one night and over some stupid thing we got in a wrestling match that was not, like, a friendly wrestling match. In the middle of the Harvard Bridge, in the snow, at like two in the morning."[4] But eventually the friendship became more equal. It had to, because the two would eventually go into business together and turn themselves into multimillionaires.

After a successful run at Harvard, Bannon nevertheless was having trouble scoring a job. He discovered that many investment banks considered him too old to stamp with their own image; his Navy service was held against him for similar reasons; and he had not gone to the right prep schools or right undergraduate university. As Bannon tells it, one day he was at a Goldman Sachs recruitment event overflowing with job candidates. Based on past experience, he felt he had no chance at getting selected. But, to pass the time, he struck up a conversation about baseball with two random young men. One, as it turned out, was John Weinberg Jr., whose father ran Goldman Sachs, and the other was Rob Kaplan, a future senior partner at the firm. After the event, when the recruiters were going over the candidates, Bannon was quickly dismissed as too old, but Weinberg and Kaplan intervened, said he was a great guy, based on their conversation with him, and suddenly he was in.[5]

Bannon joined Goldman in 1985, during the era of Michael Milken, junk bonds, and hostile takeovers. He took up residence in the mergers and acquisitions department, where it was his job to figure out how to defend the firm's clients against corporate raiders.[6] With Bannon's backing, Vorse was hired by Goldman too, though he worked in a different division. After a few years, Goldman sent Bannon out to Hollywood to try to drum up new business.

Bannon had earned a reputation for industriousness in college and his nose hit the grindstone even harder now with Goldman Sachs. He and Vorse, who initially stayed in New York, were working hundred-hour weeks. "At Harvard business school people would say there are few people who worked harder than he did. When he got to Goldman Sachs—there are few people who worked harder than he did. I think he really enjoys it." If anything, Bannon worked even harder after Vorse and he went into business together at the end of 1989 in Los Angeles. "What you would think of as a vacation—I don't know if he's ever been on a vacation like that," Vorse said. "Maybe over the years he's been on two- or three-day things," but that was about it.[7]

Bannon's competitive advantage was not only that he could out-think most people, but he would outwork them too. "Nothing in this world can take the place of persistence," Calvin Coolidge once said. "Nothing is more common than unsuccessful men with talent." No one ever accused Stephen Bannon of a lack of persistence. His capacity for work was phenomenal, his apparent need for sleep minimal. He was almost always working.

In Vorse's telling, Bannon & Co., which Bannon started with Vorse and two other partners—and which was eventually winnowed down to just the two of them—focused on a group of about thirty small, independent film and production companies, which were in financial trouble because they had taken loans they couldn't service. Bannon's firm worked on making deals for the ailing companies, finding buyers or investors.

Vorse and Bannon developed a "framework and a methodology" to better determine the value of these companies. They realized that the usual measures of assets and operations could disguise wide variations in value, rather as an aerial view of a housing development of similarly sized houses would miss internal variations like an indoor pool or a remodeled kitchen. For instance, not all B-movies held by a distribution company were created equal. Some came with potentially valuable subsidiary rights, especially in overseas markets. Bannon's firm not only analyzed assets and operations, but thoroughly parsed the interrelated balance sheets, income statements, and cash flow. "Nobody [else] spent the time" to do this, said Vorse; "I mean nobody." Bannon and Vorse did the hard work other companies didn't; and it paid off. They earned a reputation as a firm that made the most reliable, accurate, and trustworthy assessments of companies so that investors and buyers would know exactly what they were acquiring. When it came to this sort of analysis, Vorse said, "We were the best."

Bannon was the big thinker, the strategist, the business development guy. Vorse was the tactician, evaluating Bannon's deals and nailing down the details. Bannon would meet with anyone. "I'd see someone walk in with their dog," said Vorse. "I would see people of every religion, sex, race, socioeconomic status. It wasn't like Steve said, 'Okay, what's the pedigree on that person before I meet him.' He was meeting with everybody. He's not close-minded in any way." Some of the ideas were off the wall, Vorse said, "but there was a thought process. And there was a logic to them." Bannon was an optimist and wanted to make ideas work. And if he thought there were possibilities, he'd bring Vorse in. "We used to laugh that it wasn't. 'I was half empty and he was half full,' it was 'I was half empty and he was overflowing,'" Vorse said.[8]

Bannon was a tough and driven boss, according to Chris Bannon, who also worked with him at Bannon & Co. "He'd set unreasonable timelines," Chris said. "He wanted to be better than anybody else who came in the door who just said, 'Oh, I'll get that to you in two weeks.' Steve's competitive advantage was, 'We will work around the clock for six days and deliver it by Wednesday. I'm gonna do a better job and I'm gonna do it faster.'" And he expected the same of those who worked for him. *Problem with your kid? Not my problem. Where are the deliverables?*

It was during this time that the Bannon whiteboard emerged. Bannon is known today for having kept a whiteboard in his office in the White House, where he listed each of Trump's campaign promises and checked them off as they were accomplished. "We were big into the whiteboard—think things through, hash things out, and see what makes sense and what doesn't," said Vorse. When he wasn't intensely pacing the room during meetings, Bannon would study and amend the whiteboard.

★

The company's most famous deal happened in 1993. Vorse and Bannon helped represent Westinghouse in a deal to sell its stake in

Castle Rock Entertainment, a film and TV production company, to Ted Turner. The pair advised Westinghouse to take less money but retain a participation in the syndication of five Castle Rock television shows. As part of the deal, Bannon and Vorse would get a piece of the action. At least one of the shows, they felt, had some potential, though they couldn't say for sure it would be a hit. The show was a modestly successful program about to enter its fifth season. It was called *Seinfeld*.

"I think it was just the risk-reward trade off," Vorse said of the rationale for the deal. "It was not a lot of money that they were giving up in exchange for that," he noted. "And by the way, it was their decision," he said of Westinghouse, careful not to take too much credit. "Nobody knew that it would be like it is, but there was the inkling that *Seinfeld* had some potential."

It did. That year it jumped from number twenty-five in the Nielsen ratings to number three. For the next four years, it was either first or second. By the time it signed off at number one in 1998, it was clear that years of syndication money would be rolling in.

In late 1993, Bannon was involved in another famous deal: saving the troubled Biosphere 2 project in Oracle, Arizona. The Biosphere was meant to test the survivability of people, animals, and plants in a closed environment of the sort that might be created if we colonized other planets. Unfortunately, the animals and plants were dying, and the people were suffering. "Of 150 species of carefully selected insects, all disappeared except cockroaches and a species of Arizona ant," a newspaper reported at the time, and the cockroaches and ants were not just thriving, they were taking over the Biosphere. "When Bannon led a VIP group in after the first Biospherians came out, there were so many of these insects inside that 'the floor looked like it was moving.'"[9] The Biosphere project was losing a cool $1 million a month, and something drastic had to be done to save it.

Bannon decided that the project needed the backing of a large institution. He eventually hooked up with an official from Columbia University who decided the giant enclosed area would be a perfect way to test the effects of global warming. Owner Edward Bass fired the existing management and put Steve Bannon in charge in the spring of 1994. "The whole mentality has got to change— this is not a space ship, it's a cyclotron," Bannon declared.[10]

In a January 13, 1995, C-SPAN interview, Bannon, sporting an open-collar blue shirt and a green cotton jacket that looks like he grabbed it off the rack at Patagonia or REI, can be seen touting the Biosphere for environmental scientists. "What a lot of the scientists who are studying global change and studying the effects of greenhouse gases—many of them feel that the Earth's atmosphere in a hundred years is what the Biosphere 2's atmosphere is today," Bannon earnestly advises. "The power of this place is allowing those scientists who are really involved in study of global change... really have to work with just computer simulation. This actually allows them to study and monitor the impact of enhanced CO_2 and other greenhouse gases on humans, plants, and in animals."[11]

Ironically enough, Bannon would later became a global warming skeptic and one of the driving forces behind President Trump's withdrawal from the Paris climate accord.

Bannon's experience at Biosphere was not entirely happy. Many will attest that Bannon is a tough and demanding boss and can be aggressive, quick-tempered, and swear like a sailor. After Margret Augustine was fired as CEO and Bannon took over, a couple of Biosphere 2 employees, loyal to the old regime, actually broke into the Biosphere to warn crew members about the change of command and were subsequently fired. One of them, Abigail Alling, faced criminal charges related to the break in. She and the other former employee sued Biosphere 2 for breach of contract. In the civil trial, Bannon admitted he "vowed to kick [Alling's] ass" and also to take a statement she had written about the safety problems at Biosphere 2 and "ram it down her fucking throat." And he called her a "bimbo." But the jury also got a laugh and a taste of why the place had needed new management in the first place. Augustine was questioned during a deposition about Biosphere 2 activities during the last quarter of a fiscal year. "What is a last quarter?' asked Augustine.[12] While Steve Bannon no longer has any connection to the Biosphere project, Chris Bannon does, working on it part-time, under the auspices of the University of Arizona, which now runs it.

In the mid-1990s, Bannon and Vorse represented PolyGram as it acquired most of the small production and distribution companies that were Bannon & Co.'s bread and butter. They worked for PolyGram again when it was sold to Seagram Company. In November 1996, they formed a strategic alliance with the French bank Société Générale. Two years later, they sold their firm to the bank, and stayed on to run their division for another two years before they departed. By then they had plenty of money. Vorse retired for fifteen years.

But Bannon kept working a hundred hours a week.

*

Bannon's brutal work ethic and his drive for deals and success seem to have been born as much out of a determination to succeed and win as it was a desire to get rich. Although he hardly minded becoming rich, friends, associates, and family members describe him as a man who shuns ostentatious displays of wealth. As a businessman, his uniform was more preppy than Wall Street. He was known as "a no-socks-and-loafers kind of guy."[13] Though pressed into jackets and ties during his White House job by his red-tie-and-dark-blue-suit boss, Bannon's outfit of choice today tends to involve cargo shorts or khakis and a pair of collared shirts, oddly layered one on top of the other. The townhouse on Capitol Hill where he still spends time is known as the "Breitbart Embassy," having served as a workplace for his website's staff. The front area and dining room have a faded feel—one can imagine it might once have been a nineteenth-century Washington belle's salon, festooned with flowers and fresh paint, but it certainly shows its age now. There doesn't outwardly seem to be anything particularly fancy about the building or about the man who would come home there from the White House.

Chris said that once Steve left Ginter Park and saw how others higher up the income scale lived, he thought he might have some of that too, thank you very much. "It was almost segregation—middle-class knucklehead Irish guys not welcome. We were never around luxury so when you saw it, it was impressive." But even though Steve Bannon raked in millions during his business career, and knew luxury, he still, as Chris noted, "loves the Spartan" lifestyle. "After he got divorced he had a place on Manhattan Beach he rented. It was a duplex. A doctor owned it and Steve nicknamed it 'Sparta.' It had a chair and the light and books on the floor and a cot off the stove. It was very Steve."[14]

While stingy with himself, Bannon is quietly generous with others. One day, visiting Richmond, Bannon noticed a homeless man on the corner of Laburnum and Chamberlain, not far from his childhood home. "Steve gave him a few hundred dollars and got him a room," his sister Mary Beth said. Bannon didn't mention it. "Somebody else noticed or told us," she said.[15]

"When he started making money he would send my parents on trips," said Chris. "He'd start to pay back the things that they missed. Even our high school principal, he sent him and his sister who was sick on a whirlwind month-long trip to the West. He put them up in Sedona at the famous resort up there." Money made this possible, but Bannon had always been generous, according to his brother Chris. As tough as he Steve was, he'd nevertheless, "turn around and give you the shirt off his back."[16]

Bannon's business dealings continued to focus on the entertainment industry. In 2005, he became co-chairman of Genius Products, which distributed programming to home video retailers, cable outlets, specialty theater chains, and a direct mail catalog.[17] Genius partnered with The Weinstein Company to handle its home video releases, putting Bannon in business with the ultra-liberal Harvey Weinstein.

Bannon also took a senior role with IGE, the video game company, with the intention of taking the company public. He brought the company tens of millions of dollars of investment from private equity firms led by Goldman Sachs and helped reorganize it as Affinity Holdings. "Affinity Media Holdings stabilized under Bannon's leadership. Bannon remained chief executive of Affinity and an affiliated company called IMI Exchange until 2011," according to *The Washington Post*.[18]

Bannon said he pursued a business career because he savored the competition and coveted the freedom money could buy him. "I never did anything for the money, but I wanted to earn a lot of money for the simple reason, it's about your time," he said. "What money gives you is simply the ability to get your life back in control. Look, my dad is the greatest guy in the world, but I saw him get up every morning at 5 o'clock and come back and have very little time for the kids," he said. "The reason was he worked all day, and when he came back at night he was tired." While noting that, "The time we got was quality," Bannon decided, "I love this guy, but that's exactly what I will never do." The money, Bannon said, allowed him to pursue his own interests—and those interests were, chiefly, making movies and, increasingly, politics. He wanted to advance a conservative agenda through movies and through journalism.[19]

The movies came first. According to his friend and former Virginia Tech roommate Peter Alberice, Bannon "started writing screenplays when he was working at Goldman Sachs. And I've read a couple of them, and they were really, really good." At that time, he was interested in movies that dealt with historical themes; but that interest was shifting to the political.

In 2004, he wrote and directed a documentary that combined history and politics, *In the Face of Evil: Reagan's War in Word and Deed*. With that film, Bannon's brand of conservative populism and nationalism, which he saw expressed in his hero Reagan, came to the forefront. Bannon began to leave the world of high finance for the world of political filmmaking. "The moment he left that world [of high finance], there was a physical transformation," said conservative author Peter Schweizer, who collaborated with Bannon on several movies, including *In the Face of Evil*. He started to shed the preppy look. "The uniform of those elite institutions was gone."[20]

Taking its place was Bannon, the conservative populist rebel.

CHAPTER FIVE

The Auteur

When Bannon started making movies, his goal wasn't to make a lot of money—he already had that—it was to express and promote a point of view.

His movies aren't for everyone. Writers from *Politico* and the *Daily Beast* who say they "binge watched" Bannon's movies appear to have barely survived the experience. "Little did I know what a relentlessly soul-sucking endeavor it would be," writes Asawin Suebsaeng in a relentlessly snarky piece for the *Daily Beast*.[1] "But I did it for you, the reader." Writing for *Politico*, Adam Wren quips that, "Four documentaries into the experiment, I have to admit I wanted out. I brainstormed excuses to email my editor, begging off the assignment. But I was too far down the rabbit hole to stop." Even so, Wren took Bannon's goals as a filmmaker seriously— addressing the threats to Western civilization—but he questioned his outlook: "The first thing I learned is that in Bannon's filmic world, there are no shades of gray, only black and white, sinners and saints, demons and angels."[2]

"What I've tried to do is weaponize film," Bannon said in 2010 as he promoted his film *Fire from the Heartland* about conservative women. "I want these films to be incredibly provocative. I wanted to present our point of view. I'm not interested in saying, 'on one hand and the other.'"[3]

Bannon's films embody the two great intellectual passions of his life—history and philosophy—and, as few have noticed, reflect his service in the Navy, because an overriding theme of his films is defending America against its enemies, foreign and domestic.

Bannon's first documentary film, *In the Face of Evil: Reagan's War in Word and Deed*, won awards for "Best Documentary" of the year from the Liberty Film Festival and from the American Film Renaissance. It even caught the eye of the *New York Times*, which interviewed Bannon and identified him as one of several conservative movie makers looking to make their mark.

The *Times* story noted that "Though heavier than most on messianic zeal, Mr. Bannon—Roman Catholic filmmaker, conservative-film financier, Washington networker and Hollywood deal-chaser—is emblematic of a new wave [of conservatives] in Hollywood, a group that intends to...promote godliness, Pax Americana and its own view of family values." "We have the money, we have the ideas," Bannon told the *Times*. "What we don't have—and what the left has in spades—are great filmmakers." Bannon pointed to two movies—Mel Gibson's *The Passion of the Christ*, and *The Lord of the Rings*, which he described as "a Christian allegory"—that had done well at the box office and collected bushels of awards, and yet left the media largely unmoved. "So here you have Sodom and Gomorrah bowing to the great Christian God, and did you guys notice? No, because

99 per cent of the content in the media's sewage pipes is the culture of death, not life," Bannon said. "In the future, why wouldn't we want to take over the levers of Hollywood?" he said with what the *Times* described as a rakish grin. "We're the peasants with the pitchforks storming the lord's manor."[4]

Bannon studied the great documentary filmmakers of the past—including, controversially, the films of Leni Riefenstahl, who made some of the most celebrated documentary films of all time, but made them in support of Nazisim. He felt conservative filmmakers failed to provide their audiences with artistic quality and intellectual challenge. "The reason all the conservative documentaries suck is, we're not making [the audience] stretch," he said in 2017. "We have to make people reach, you've gotta put the bar above them. In the experience of going through it, they'll start to grow and they'll start to get it more. We have to make the actual watching of the film an experience for them."

Bannon's films often lead with one idea in the service of conveying another. For example, while *In the Face of Evil: Reagan's War in Word and Deed* is ostensibly a documentary about Ronald Reagan and why we should admire him, specifically for his victory in the Cold War, the film's point was actually something else. "It wasn't" as Bannon confessed, really "about Reagan, it was about the fight against a radical ideology, and [about] one guy as an instrument of how you do that. So the theme of the movie was what it takes for a democracy to attack a radical ideology. I did not have any interest in doing a film on the Cold War. Zero. I had an interest in showing us at the very beginning of this war [against radical Islam], because it's going to be just like how we destroyed the radical ideology of communism."[5]

Communism, in the film, is just one historical manifestation of "the Beast," a biblical term associated with the devil. "The

Beast" in the film is deployed as an allusion to communism, fascism, and Islamic extremism.

The documentary starts with the aftermath of World War I: "From this fever swamp rose a Beast, one that played upon man's yearning for a utopian solution to its abject misery, a quasi-religious criminal taking the form of a political messiah. The Beast embodied Nietzsche's will to power, stopping at nothing to achieve its ends. It fed off man's dark side, his fears, his prejudices, his ancient hatreds. Reaching out, first to convert, then turning in to destroy. That was the nature of the Beast. It came with many faces, many names: Bolshevism, fascism, communism, Nazism—Lenin, Mussolini, Hitler, Tojo, Stalin. But always and everywhere, regardless of the name or face, the goal remained the same: Control of the state and power. Power as an end unto itself."

Bannon's filmmaking is strongly colored by his Catholicism. Evil ideologies tempt man, as the devil would, pretending to be a messiah and reaching out to man's "dark side." The ideologies represent the easy way out, promising a false "utopia" while in the end leaving those who have "fallen" for it in hell instead. "The Beast too understood the power of myth. Entire countries could moved to riot or subsist in silence, to follow or revolt, to obey or disobey."

"The Beast," the narrator continues, "had always hated the same things: Religion, a free press, intellectual inquiry, artistic expression—anything that elevated or empowered the individual. And yet all who called out the Beast, naming it for what it really was, were vilified, considered reactionary, paranoid. Warmongers. Winston Churchill, vehemently opposed by both the peace movement and the British establishment, came to power as the representative of the British workers and middle class to defend Western civilization."

Reagan, the film argues, was able to defeat communism and the Soviet Union because he was impervious to the supposedly enlightened opinions that had argued in favor of appeasing the Soviets, and instead he single-mindedly pursued the goal of confronting and defeating Communist evil. Reagan "advocated a radical agenda: Challenge the Soviets everywhere, economically, politically, militarily, and especially, psychologically," the narrator tells us. The goal was not just to "coexist with the Russians, but defeat them."

"Reagan," says author Peter Schweizer in the film, "ultimately overcame the culture of fear because he refused to live by it."

Bannon says he was provoked into making the documentary because he thought Americans needed to understand, in the days after the Islamist terrorist attacks on this country on September 11, 2001, that they were in for a long war, a long ideological struggle against another enemy of Western civilization, one that would not be wished away by mere good feelings and expressions of tolerance and a desire to get back to our normal lives. "After 9/11 I saw all my New York buddies, you know, Goldman Sachs, and upper East Side guys—and guys that are dear friends—and everybody was coming together down in Washington Square park, all holding hands, singing God Bless America," he said. Soon, he knew, everyone would be faced with the reality that this was war, and "Kumbaya" wasn't going to hack it. Once the melodies had faded, the United States was going to be in an historic and epic struggle against a radical ideology that was implacably determined to destroy the West.

"I said, this [moment of unity] is going to last about six months—until we start killing a lot of bad guys, until we start killing a lot of hostiles," Bannon said. "All of a sudden...this is going to be bad."

Bannon had optioned the film rights to Peter Schweizer's book *Reagan's War* in 2002, but did not draw up plans for the documentary until he perceived it as a road map for how America should conduct a disciplined, long-term fight against radical Islam:

> I thought about, how do you actually tell the story, and then it hit me, it's Schweizer's book, it's *Reagan's War*, because what Reagan understood, what those guys understood, is it literally takes decades, maybe a hundred years, maybe longer, to defeat a radical ideology. And you are going to have good days, and you're going to have bad days. You're going to have days that you're winning, and you're going to have times that you think you're losing, but if you stick with it, and keep your mind on exactly what you're trying to accomplish, and are able to hand the baton down generation to generation, you can win....We'll be victorious as long as we stick to our principles and don't give up the fight.[6]

As the film comes to a close, it celebrates the return of religious and political freedom to the formerly captive nations of Eastern Europe and the Soviet Union, including footage of Muslims at prayer. But suddenly, an eerie coda begins.

"The wolf had not passed by the door. War had not been wished away," the narrator warns as the second plane flies into the South Tower of the World Trade Center. Rachmaninoff's "Vespers" plays elegiacally in the background. Images of Islamic extremists—their indoctrination efforts and terrorism—appear. "Reaching out, first to convert, then turning in to destroy. That was the nature of the Beast. But always and everywhere, regardless of the name or face, the goal remained the same: Control of the state and power. Power as an end unto itself."

Then the most jarring images of all: people leaping to their deaths as the towers burn. Bannon had gotten the footage, which he said was too horrifying to find in the United States, from Mexico, seeking to make the most searing statement he could. Finally, the towers collapse.

In the 2004 movie's final moments, Bannon suggests that the Islamic militants are also attacking Islam, or perverting it, reminding that "religion" was among the things "The Beast had always hated." As with Communism, some in the West responded meekly. "Civilization responded as civilization always has, by trying to wish it away, hoping the wolf would pass by the door. Peace movements, speeches, petitions, demonstrations, all tried to ward off the Beast. Cato, in his 40 years in the Senate, ended every speech with the same mantra: *Carthago delenda est*. Carthage must be destroyed."

Reagan returns to the screen: "You and I have a rendezvous with destiny. We'll preserve for our children, this, the last best hope of man on earth, or we'll sentence them to take the last step into a thousand years of darkness." As Rachmaninov's "Vespers" fades to silence, a quote appears, attributed to Reagan: "Evil is powerless if the good are unafraid."

Roll credits.

★

Bannon, in an interview in July 2017, told me that "Islam as a faith" is not a problem because he believes there are many legitimate paths for people to seek God. What we cannot avoid noticing, however, is that Islam has a problem in adapting to modernity, he said.

"The people that go after Islam *qua* Islam—it's not Islam as a faith" that is the problem, Bannon asserted. "If you study Sufism [as Bannon has done], and particularly the eternal struggle that Islam calls for, I think that's fine. It's a path to enlightenment or a path to God...just like Judaism's got its path, just like Christianity's got its path. It's not for anybody to determine what path an individual takes." The path represents an "individuals' understanding that the interior practice of the presence of God is the one thing that will separate...their [interior] life from exterior life. Everybody has to come to that through their own work."

In that regard, "Islam, in fact, has a very powerful tradition," he said. "One of the reasons for Jihad is that inner work on oneself," Bannon said, referring to the concept of an individual's internal struggle, not a rationale for attacking nonbelievers.

But Bannon adds, "It is very evident when you look at Islam, it has not had its meeting with the Enlightenment. It has not had that transition to modernity. Aspects of it—and, in fact, aspects that are taught at Madrassas and in some of these mosques throughout the world—are quite radical and quite radical in proselytizing, where no other religion can be accepted."

He notes that parts of the Islamic world have returned to the practice of forcing non-Muslims "to pay penalties...and they can never really be full citizens. That aspect is just completely counter to the modern world."[7]

This radical form of Islam, an Islam that cannot make its peace with modernity, can also, Bannon warns, not make its peace with America or with the West. Bannon's first major documentary was a warning that America needed to have faith in itself, that it needed to gird itself for another giant ideological war, and that it needed another leader, like Ronald Reagan, with the moral clarity and understanding to recognize the challenge and meet it.

CHAPTER SIX

Generation Zero

While he remained active as a producer, Bannon did not write and direct another documentary for five years after his Reagan film. He had no projects, he said, that inspired him. That changed after America's financial system collapsed in the fall of 2008. Bannon felt that the financial tremors were "going to be massive" and that the aftershocks would include dramatic change—and not just in the economy.[1] He also had a new business partner who wanted to work with him on film projects.

David Bossie was a forty-three-year-old conservative activist who had volunteered for Ronald Reagan's 1984 reelection campaign as a teen and then never looked back. Bossie had made a specialty of investigating the Clintons, and by the mid-1990s, he was serving as the chief investigator for former Congressman Dan Burton's House Oversight Committee, aggressively probing Bill Clinton's dubious campaign finances. But he was forced to resign after eighteen months following an outcry over what critics said was selective editing of the jailhouse tapes of a Clinton associate, Webster Hubbell. In 2001, Bossie became president of a conservative nonprofit called Citizens United, where he produced the 2008 documentary film *Hillary: The Movie*, a guided tour of the many political scandals dogging Mrs. Clinton. It was scheduled to air on TV before a series of Democratic primaries, but the Federal Election Commission banned the film, ruling that it was essentially a corporate-funded campaign ad that, under the McCain-Feingold campaign reform act, could not be broadcast during election season. Citizens United's challenge to the ruling led to the landmark Supreme Court decision that said the government had no business under the First Amendment banning corporate spending during elections.

As they discussed film projects, Bannon told Bossie he wanted to make a film about the collapse of America's financial system, but to do so as part of an even larger story, which would include how America's financial elite had abused America's workers and how American culture was changing for the worse, largely because of self-indulgent Baby Boomers who were destroying the American Dream.

"Narcissism," Bannon told Fox News host Sean Hannity later, when he was promoting the film, was the root cause of the financial collapse, the narcissism of the "Me Generation" that puts self above others, easy money over real value, and political correctness over reality; narcissism, hedonism, selfishness, and greed—sins that Bannon recognized as such from his deeply ingrained Catholicism—had reaped their whirlwind in the banks and financial markets, and endangered America's future.

Bannon had long been convinced that history moves in cycles, and after he read the 1997 book *The Fourth Turning* by William

Strauss and Neil Howe, which had accurately predicted an economic crisis, he incorporated their insights into his vision of what had happened.

According to Strauss and Howe, history revolves in cycles lasting approximately eighty to a hundred years, what the authors term a "saeculum." Each saeculum is divided into four "turnings" lasting about twenty to twenty-five years. Each turning has specific characteristics driven by the personalities of four distinct types of generations and the age of the generations during each turning. In short, the First Turning is a time of relative prosperity and stability in which adults subscribe to traditional values, conformity is emphasized, and children are protected and indulged by parents who have just survived the horror of the great crisis that attends each saeculum—generally war or economic strife—and don't want their little ones to experience discomfort or pain. Think, for example, of the postwar period extending through the 1950s and into the early 1960s and parents who had lived, either as children or young adults, through the Depression and World War II. That period is the "First Turning" of the current "saeculum."

Parents with children during the First Turning, of course, expect that their kids will grow up to be obedient and happy, filled with gratitude for all they've been given. A house in the suburbs, a big car in the driveway, and a chunk of tasty meat broiled in a modern kitchen and deposited on the dinner table—who could want anything more? Well-fed, air-conditioned, and entertained by television, the Baby Boomers were headed for lives of comfort and complacency.

Until all that became as dull as a Levittown white picket fence. The search for "meaning" began, as the Boomers grew to question the value system within which they had been raised.

Strauss and Howe define those born during a First Turning and coming to adulthood during a Second Turning (the Baby Boomers in this case) as a "prophet generation." With creature comforts provided for and cash in their pockets, their quest becomes intellectual and spiritual. Many Baby Boomers followed Timothy Leary's advice to "turn on, tune in, and drop out," or accepted that such self-absorption and irresponsibility were actually higher values. Bannon sees these values as bankrupt, and in his 2010 movie *Generation Zero*, he also blames them for eventually bankrupting the American financial system as they grew to middle age.

Bannon told Bossie that he wanted to get his points across in an unusual way, incorporating rapid cuts, discordant music, and jarring, often harrowing, images. Bossie didn't, at first, understand what Bannon was driving at, but Bannon said, "Just bear with me," and Bossie did.[2]

Bannon's approach in *Generation Zero* makes it a morbidly compelling, if not particularly pleasant, film to watch—and the message gets through unmistakably. In the film, conservative scholar Victor Davis Hanson tells us that the habits and traditional moral values of the 1950s "were pedestrian protocols, and they were easy to caricature. But slowly over time, they create the stuff of civilization."[3] Many in the prophet generation rebelled against that civilization.

Bannon captures the generational conflict within 1960s America by juxtaposing Neil Armstrong and Buzz Aldrin's 1969 landing on the moon with the 1969 hippie rock concert in Woodstock, New York. The moon landing was the result of discipline, technology, and a sense of duty and purpose that reflected 1950s values. Woodstock, however, according to *Time* magazine's coverage of the event, was "the proclamation of a new set of values. The pleasure principle has been elevated over the Puritan ethic of work. To do one's own thing is a greater duty than to be a useful citizen....The children of plenty have voiced an intention to live by a different ethical standard than their parents accepted."

These leftist, "counterculture" values, which Baby Boomers often embraced, or at least indulged, represent, Bannon believes, a real civilizational threat, because in every civilization "You're only one or two generations away from losing everything."[4] Bannon cited Ronald Reagan's famous 1964 speech, "A Time for Choosing," as underlining that point. He also quoted another speech Reagan gave in 1961 where he said, "Freedom is never more than one generation away from extinction. We didn't pass it to our children in the bloodstream. It must be fought for, protected, and handed on for them to do the same, or one day we will spend our sunset years telling our children and our children's children what it was once like in the United States where men were free."[5]

In *Generation Zero*, Catholic theologian and conservative philosopher Michael Novak laments that the Baby Boomer generation, particularly the wealthiest and most privileged among them, decoupled American culture from its past. "One of the awful things that happened in the 1960s was the sense—that phrase you can't trust anybody over thirty. What it meant was you can't trust any civilization beyond our present time horizon," Novak said. "Immediately, we lost our connection with the past. It was a betrayal by the elites. I wonder if it has any precedent in history, when a generation so turned off the light switch to the past."[6]

But Bannon's film suggests something even darker was at work, that the self-indulgence, the denial of history, were encouraged by elites who had other plans in mind. There were elements on the Left who consciously wanted to bankrupt America in order to "reform" it in the socialist fashion they desired. *Generation Zero* references in particular Richard Cloward and Frances Fox Piven.

The narrator tells us that many on the Left believed that the "only way you can change an evil society is to bankrupt that society. And two professors at Columbia University, Cloward and Piven, developed such a strategy called the crisis strategy. The essence of the Cloward and Piven strategy was to sabotage and destroy the capitalist system by creating bureaucratic demands, excessive regulations, and entitlements that would lead to economic ruin, economic collapse, and bankruptcy. Once you've reached that point of bankruptcy, that society is ripe for revolutionary change."

The Left has now for two decades had the means to effect such a plan. From the film: "By the late 1990s, the Left had taken over many of the institutions of power, meaning government, media, and academe, and it was from these places and positions of power that they were able to disrupt the system and implement a strategy that was designed to ultimately undermine the capitalist system." By 1971, the "community organizer" Saul Alinsky had published *Rules for Radicals*, a how-to guide for leftists to gain power and topple what they believed was a fundamentally evil, racist, and sexist society. Among Alinsky's most famous acolytes were Hillary Clinton and Barack Obama.

Bannon recognizes that the Left had succeeded to a greater degree than most people realize. America's economic system is already bankrupt by any reasonable definition. Barack Obama added about $10 trillion in debt to the approximately $10 trillion he inherited—and that was while cutting defense spending by hundreds of billions of dollars.[7] Over the course of the next three generations, taxpayers will have to find another $49 trillion to fund Social Security and Medicare entitlements.[8]

A sizable amount of America's debt, and the beginning of its rapid expansion, occurred during the period of Strauss and Howe's "Third Turning," which stretched from about 1984 until the mid-2000s, and into the "Fourth Turning," which began as Barack Obama became president. By this time, irresponsible Boomers had ascended to positions of power and were squandering the nation's wealth. The "Prophet Generation" decided it could solve the nation's problems by massively increasing the size of government. And since there wasn't enough money to confiscate from their fellow citizens, they borrowed what they needed.

"The forgotten man today is our children and grandchildren. Because we're taking their money and we're leaving them with the debt. The grandparents are robbing the grandchildren," says one of the film's narrators.

Adds another: "This sense, that there was no risk, that there was no mountain we couldn't climb—that same generation created financial Armageddon, not just for themselves but their children, their children's children, and they wiped out 200 years of financial responsibility for their ancestors, all in about 20 years."

Bannon told a cheerful young interviewer on "Gen Y TV" in 2011, "You have the unfortunate problem of having to pay for a baby boom that came before you, but you're not gonna really have anybody in back of you who is able to pick up the tab for your own."

Bannon warned: "Unless this discussion changes rapidly...your generation...[will] be [financially] wiped out even before it starts."

That generation gave its name to the movie, *Generation Zero*.

In a speech in 2011, Bannon said: "This [debt] crisis is of such a magnitude, it's unprecedented in our country's history, and unprecedented in the world's history. We had some pretty sizable enemies in the 20th century: Hitler, Mussolini, the military junta in Japan, the Kaiser, Lenin, Mao, Stalin—you know, you go on and on and on. These guys couldn't even envision what we had done to ourselves...." The problem went far deeper than one spendthrift president, he said. "Barack Obama is not the problem. Barack Obama is a symptom of a problem."[9]

*

In the Strauss and Howe model, the Third Turning is when the new values of the Second Turning begin to supplant the old civic order. One result is a fragmented culture. Individualism and eventually alienation displace community. Trust in civic institutions declines, and potential solutions to seemingly intractable problems are put off for another day. This Third Turning covers American society during the decades of the 1980s and 1990s. Strauss and Howe posit that only a terrifying crisis can end this social "unraveling." If the society unites and meets the crisis, it can survive and institute a new consensus. This is the Fourth Turning, an era marked by an economic disaster and war. And there is no escaping it.

"History is seasonal, and winter is coming," Straus and Howe warned in 1997. "Like nature's winter, the saecular winter can come early or late. A Fourth Turning can be long and difficult, brief but severe, or (perhaps) mild. But like winter, it cannot be averted. It must come in its turn."

Past Fourth Turnings featured the Revolutionary War, the Civil War, and the Depression and World War II, each of which were about eighty to a hundred years apart. If the current Fourth Turning started around 2008, when the financial crisis occurred, another large-scale war is to be expected within the next dozen years.

Strauss and Howe, writing ten years before the financial crisis and during a Third Turning, forecast "a downward economic spiral" stemming from the irresponsible habits of the Baby Boomers. "Some unforeseeable happenstance could spark a precipitous market selloff, as old investors will want to liquidate their equities to a shrinking universe of buyers," they write. "Years of savings could vanish in matter of days—or hours."

That's precisely what happened. At one point, during the financial collapse of 2008–2009, the Dow Jones lost half its value, and among those who lost most of his savings was Bannon's father Martin.

According to *Generation Zero*, the 2008 financial crash was the result of risky lending practices, encouraged by big government, embraced by big banks, and supported by big business, a cabal of irresponsible elites who thought only of themselves. "We have big government, and we have big finance, and big business that merged and became joined at the hip," says Peter Schweizer in the film. "We have a system today where elites are joined together and have the ability to transform or direct American society to almost any direction that they want to."

Bannon does not believe investment bankers are inherently evil. But he does believe that the rules changed, for the worse, as did the character of the people running the banks. "The investment banks are incredibly important in the post-war era, an integral part of the building of the United States to industrial power," Steve Bannon told Sean Hannity in an interview to promote *Generation Zero*. "Goldman Sachs, Morgan Stanley, First Boston—these were partnerships with men that have fought in the Second World War and put their country first and had tremendous fiduciary responsibility."

Unlike socialist critics of the bankers, Bannon wasn't bothered by their eagerness to make money. Bannon had made plenty of that himself. It was their abnegation of responsibility to the country, to the people to who had entrusted them with their cash, and the workers who trusted the elites to be responsible stewards of the economy. "Goldman Sachs represented excellence and meritocracy," he said in an appearance in *Goldman Sachs: The Bank That Runs the World*, a 2012 French documentary. "It didn't matter where you came from, it didn't matter what school you went to, what your religion was or what was your ethnicity," he said. "It just mattered how hard you worked, how smart you were, and how good a banker you were for your clients. It was really like joining the Jesuits."

During the 1990s and 2000s, however, leadership at banks like Goldman Sachs was handed down to elite Baby Boomers who brought the self-indulgence of Woodstock to Wall Street. All businessmen and bankers want to make a buck. The difference with this new generation was that they didn't care if anyone else suffered in the process.

Before 1970, investment banks were partnerships. As partnerships, if one of the partners lost money, everyone was responsible for the financial consequences. That is, you had some incentive to invest conservatively and not expose too much of your portfolio to high risk because, to use a technical term, your ass was on the line. In 1970, some investment banks started to go public, which meant shareholders bore the responsibility for losses. And ultimately, as became apparent in 2008, taxpayers did too. During the following decades, Merrill Lynch, Bear Stearns, Lehman Brothers, and Morgan Stanley all became publicly owned. Goldman Sachs did not shed its partnership restraints until 1999, well after Bannon had left.[10]

The egalitarian-minded Boomers demanded that bankers lend money to minorities and other "oppressed" groups to buy houses, regardless of their ability to afford a house. And in many cases, those who took the loans had no greater sense of responsibility than the financial jackals who were preying on them. Banks had sought and were granted greater "leverage" to lend vast sums to people who had only a little bit of skin in the game, according to the film. With partnerships dissolved and responsibility transferred to shareholders, who cared? And once banks lost their lunch money they came crying to daddy, whose name was Hank Paulson, George W. Bush's Treasury secretary. Paulson, himself a former poobah at Goldman Sachs, decided to fix the financiers' mistakes by laying the costs on taxpayers. Paulson got Congress to authorize $700 billion to purchase "troubled assets," which de facto passed all the bad debt, until it was eventually repaid, onto the American people who responsibly saved their money and paid their taxes.

That the investment banks were saved by government intervention was emblematic for Bannon of the country's cultural decline, its self-indulgent rejection of personal responsibility, and worst of all, the willingness of the elites to put their interests over those of working men and women, the middle class. The middle class was getting squeezed between a growing underclass reliant on government handouts, and the wealthy bankers and corporate big wheels who lobbied the government to fatten their profits and bail them out if they screwed up.

"We have two systems in this country. We have socialism for the very poor. We have socialism for the wealthy. We have capitalism for the middle class," Bannon said during his appearance on Hannity's show. "The investment banking part of this meltdown is very important. That's what people really don't understand. And it is a bail-out of the financial elites. And it's really socialism."

Neil Howe says in *Generation Zero* that irresponsible Baby Boomers "have led us, late in the Third Turning, to a very dangerous situation." That danger is not just the financial collapse of 2008, but given that America is into the Fourth Turning, perhaps a major military conflict.

Bannon, however, as a believer in the Catholic doctrine of free will, does not believe in historical inevitabilities even if he does believe in general historical cycles. "We're in the Fourth Turning of American history, I don't think there's any doubt about that," Bannon told me in July 2017. "Now, does that mean there's going to be a cataclysmic war? The answer is, I don't think so, but I can't foretell history."[11]

The real question for Bannon is what type of society will be forged from the Fourth Turning, around what values will Americans unite and find a consensus? "I don't know what the outcome will be," he said. "We're going to be one thing or the other on the other side of this. We're either going to be the America that we remember in the height of its greatness, when it depended upon itself and it depended upon its people—and the institutions of this country thought about the working people of this country in the golden age after World War II—or we'll be something totally different. I think we were heading down the path of something totally different." And that, Bannon said, is why he decided to get involved in political movements and ultimately get behind the candidacy of Donald Trump, who was, he says, "an agent of change."[12]

When Donald Trump said he wanted to make America great again, he had an ally in Steve Bannon.

CHAPTER SEVEN

A Flawed Visionary

Steve Bannon's success in business and public life has not always been matched by success in his private life. His marriage to Susie Houff ended in divorce. He married his second wife, Mary Louise Piccard, just days before she gave birth to their twins in 1995.[1] In 1996, Piccard filed a domestic violence report against Bannon (the case was dismissed),[2] and in 1997, Piccard and Bannon began a bitter divorce battle that lasted ten years.[3] He married for a third time, to Tea Party activist Diane Clohesy, and was divorced again in 2009. While Steve Bannon ascended professional heights his father never dreamed of, he failed at what his father did superlatively well, holding together a nuclear family.

He has, however, managed to stay on good terms with his first wife, Susie, who is also friendly with his siblings and father. And Bannon is extremely close to his daughter Maureen, a West Point graduate who served in Iraq.

At West Point, Maureen was a star of the volleyball team, and he became a fanatical fan, sending her statistics to friends (Maureen was a three-time Patriot League Setter of the Year and four-time all-league honoree), attending nearly every match (Maureen's mother often attended as well), just as earlier in her life, Bannon logged thousands of miles flying from business trips to help coach her in basketball.

"It's such a comforting feeling having my parents there," Maureen Bannon said in a profile piece for the West Point athletics website. "Whether I'm on the road or in Gillis Field House, my dad is always there. There's a feeling that somebody is always behind me, whether I'm having a great match or struggling through a rough one."

The profile notes that "Growing up in a split-family environment, along with a job that required her father to travel much of the time, Bannon rarely saw her dad on a regular basis. He's made up for it, however, cheering on his daughter and supporting the Black Knights' program in over 100 matches in less than four years. He has traveled to Korea and back numerous times this season, simply to catch his daughter's team in action. 'My dad was gone a lot when I was younger, traveling all over the world for work,' Bannon said. 'But he's more than making up for it now. He's always there in my corner.'"[4]

When she graduated in 2010 and became a member of the 101st Airborne Division of the Army, his pride overflowed. In speeches he gave at the time, he characteristically began by mentioning "my pride and joy" Maureen. More recently, Maureen has said she's "nothing but proud" of her father, adding, "It disappoints me to see him being tainted as something that he's not...."[5]

As for his second wife, Mary Louise Piccard, Bannon spokeswoman Alexandra Preate told *Politico* (which had done an exposé of Piccard's accusations of domestic abuse): "The bottom line is he has a great relationship with [their] twins, he has a great relationship with the ex-wife, he still supports them."[6]

Likewise, it appears Bannon has continued to support his third wife, Diane Clohesy. She is listed as a social media manager for Breitbart News and, as has been reported, he has provided her with "emotional and financial" support when she's needed it in recent years.[7]

Bannon adores his father and is close with his immediate family. Despite his grueling schedule, he still calls his dad several times a week, and Bannon's relatives regularly land in the Washington area to have a brief visit with him. Like his mother, he keeps tabs on what everyone is doing, and, as his sister Sharon told me, "He challenges you to do better."

That's true not only with his family, but with his many friends, who cover a wide social spectrum. "Steve loves guys who are competitive and he loves interesting guys," Chris said. "He collects people. They run the entire gamut."

Scot Vorse, his former business partner and Harvard Business School buddy, said Bannon is not the sort to talk about his own problems, but will definitely listen to yours, and is "very supportive but in a candid way....He'll give you his advice whether you want it or not....Steve gives unvarnished advice and unvarnished opinions." But he added, "He's a listener. He listens very, very carefully," and he remembers friends and their family members, and is always curious about their progress.

As a boss or manager, Bannon can be loyal, supportive, and helpful, but also tough, or some say, even abusive.

"When he has opinions he'll give them and he's not shy about giving opinions," Vorse said. "But he's someone who, if he trusts you and your opinion, he will really, really rely on it and not be so stubborn. He and I had different strengths and when it was my strength, he very much deferred to it."

But if you "messed up," Bannon wasn't the type to just say "let's go to lunch" and forget about it. "He'd say, 'Hey, you screwed that up. You've got to do better tomorrow,'" Vorse said. "One of his favorite phrases is, 'That's a bunch of happy talk.' He's a pretty cut and dry, results-driven person. No, he's a *very* cut and dry, results-driven person. He'd say, 'You've got to get better. You've got to fix it. And I'm going to help you.'"

Some who worked for Bannon at Breitbart News found him abrasive or worse. "Many former employees of Breitbart News are afraid of Steve Bannon," wrote Ben Shapiro, who had served as Breitbart's editor-at-large. "He is a vindictive, nasty figure, infamous for verbally abusing supposed friends and threatening enemies."[8]

"He is someone who is prone to a lot of tirades and acts as a bully. If anyone thought Corey Lewandowski was challenging that way, wait 'til someone gets a curse-laden phone call from Steve at any hour," said former Breitbart spokesman Kurt Bardella after Bannon had taken the reins of the Trump campaign.[9]

Both Bardella and Shapiro resigned in March 2016 after they felt Bannon failed to stand up for Michelle Fields, a Breitbart reporter whose arm had been grabbed by then-Trump campaign manager Lewandowski. Shapiro, despite what would appear to be a deeply negative opinion of Bannon, worked for him for four years at Breitbart. Bardella had worked with Bannon for two years.[10]

Other Breitbart employees acknowledged that while Bannon wasn't an easy boss, he got results and helped Breitbart grow into one of the largest news sites on the Internet. Breitbart's editor-in-chief Alex Marlow said that Bannon offered a "tough love" approach that reporters often need. "Steve Bannon is one of the top political and media visionaries working anywhere, and he may be the foremost populist intellectual in the world," Marlow said. "His energy is infectious, and he's been an invaluable mentor to me."[11]

Breitbart Texas editor Brandon Darby said Bannon "is a tough boss who has shepherded me to heights I never thought I would see, largely because of that toughness and his loyalty."

And reporter Dan Riehl said Bannon was there for him when he became seriously ill. "During my five-plus years of working with Breitbart, I experienced a serious illness resulting in complex heart surgery and as CEO, Steve Bannon stood by me when many employers wouldn't have, including continuing to pay me during an extended period of time when I simply couldn't perform my normal workflow," Riehl said. "He was also quick to inquire as to how I was doing during those periods and to continue doing so as I eased my way back into work."[12]

Bannon himself acknowledges that his voice was known to rise a few decibels, but that he has worked to curb his outbursts. "I still get angry," he said. "But you know what's so interesting? I don't think I've yelled at anybody since I went on the campaign. I used to be a screamer."[13]

A detailed, on-the-mark description of Bannon comes from James Delingpole, the popular British Breitbart columnist. Writing in *The Spectator*, Delingpole noted that "A lot of Breitbart's success is down to its former executive chairman Stephen K. Bannon (aka the Steve Monster; aka Honey Badger), a truly terrifying figure: ex-US Navy; ex-Goldman Sachs; ex-movie industry, where he made a fortune accidentally buying up the rights to *Seinfeld*; infamous for his short temper and epically foul-mouthed outbursts. But though I found him petrifying to work for—he's like the eye of Sauron: he sees everything and exists on Diet Coke and no sleep—

he's probably the most impressive galvanizing force and greatest political visionary I have ever met."

As Delingpole tells it, "When we first met a bit over three years ago, he had it all planned out: he was going to destroy the corrupt, sclerotic, self-serving political establishment which he utterly despised—squishy, centrist conservatives even more than lefties—and the first stepping stone towards achieving this would be securing Britain's exit from the European Union. Thereafter, he'd capture the US presidency."

Naturally, Delingpole thought that was absurdly over-ambitious, "But look where he is now: newly appointed 'chief strategist and senior counsellor' to the next president of the USA." Bannon, Delingpole noted, "did an awful lot of groundwork on Breitbart's daily radio show on Sirius FM, engaging with and building Trump's voter base even before Trump's presidential campaign was really a thing....Bannon would talk to them like an impatient, irascible professor trying to get the very best out of students he knew were much cleverer than they realized. More often than not he was proved right."[14]

Delingpole's take captured Bannon well—a brilliant, flawed visionary. Part of that vision came from his Catholic faith—and though that faith might sometimes seem more intellectual (providing a coherent philosophy of life) than lived in Bannon's case, given his three divorces and temper tantrums, it's well to remember the old saying that the Catholic Church is a hospital for sinners rather than a museum for saints; and it has most definitely served that purpose for Steve Bannon.

CHAPTER EIGHT

Stone Cold Spiritual

One day in 1998, Bannon, as he often did, grabbed the noon flight from London to Los Angeles. He tried to return every weekend to LA from Europe in order to coach the basketball team of his daughter Maureen, the child he had had with Susie, whom he had divorced. Having sold Bannon & Co. to Société Générale, he was now working for them in London at Hambros, a grand old British institution that had just been purchased by the French bank. He had been out late drinking with clients the night before and was now nursing his hangover with a thick tuft of the hair of the dog that bit him. Sitting in first class, Bannon was gulping down a series of Bloody Marys and bubbly flutes of terribly expensive champagne. He got to his beautiful home on the beach in Los Angeles at around 9:00 p.m.—early morning London time—and opened up the fridge, where he noticed a six-pack of St. Pauli Girls. He had to coach Maureen's game at 8:00 a.m. the next morning. Well, there was still time before bed, so he drank five of them. There was one left, beckoning not to be left behind. Bannon looked at the lone remaining beer. And then, he stopped. And he began to think.

Bannon had been drinking since high school. "Being Irish Catholic, coming out of a military prep school, your manliness was tied to how much you drink." Hanging out with the guys—and drinking with them—was something Bannon enjoyed almost more than anything else. Sure, he loved dating women and was dedicated to his work, but the "centerpiece" of his life was the joy of male bonding over beers, "just laughing your ass off," he said. His drinking was fostered by the all-male environment at Benedictine, the majority-male environment of Virginia Tech, and then, of course, the Navy, where sailors often got as drunk as sailors. Bannon said he was "legendary" for going onshore and partying for days at a time. He had cooled down a bit once he got to Goldman Sachs, its hundred-hour workweeks leaving little time for booze. He ratcheted it back up again when he established his own firm.

But once he went to Paris and then to London to work for Société Générale, he started to consume alcohol at a new level of intensity. The allure of the drinking culture in Europe and its custom of combining alcohol with business was catnip for Bannon. At Hambros, Bannon recalled, they had "like five beautiful dining rooms, and every day is lunches you bring your clients to. That's what they do, and these lunches go on for like three hours," he said. "They're talking business but they drink—I'd never had a drink at lunch, and they've got these fabulous wines, then at 5 o'clock they all knock off. But it's not a New York City environment at all. New York City, you're working late. At 5 o'clock in London, they're going to a club for drinks. And they usually go to two or three places for drinks then you go later for dinner and there's more drinking. It's like you're sauced all the time."

Now back in LA, with his final St. Pauli Girl waiting for him, Bannon first took a look in the mirror and reflected on what Europe was doing to him. "I've been into this maybe two months now, and I look at myself—and by the way I'm 40 pounds lighter than I am today—but I look at myself, and I go, 'I look like shit, and I feel like shit.'"[1]

He decided to have the beer. But he also decided it would be the last one he would ever have.

The next day, a Saturday, he didn't feel too great. Sunday, he felt a little better and hopped the red-eye back to London. He hasn't had anything to drink in nearly twenty years.

Bannon had been functioning at a high level despite the booze. It seems he hid the problem well, at least from those who weren't participating in it with him. "I don't know if I've ever seen Steve drunk," said Scot Vorse, who not only went to Harvard with Bannon but spent a decade in business with him. "I know I've never seen Steve take a drug. And we were together a lot."[2]

Even if others didn't notice, Bannon did. "I started to realize in the late '80s, early '90s that it was definitely having an impact on me, on just my ability to perform," Bannon said. But he nevertheless suggests he wasn't quite an alcoholic. "I didn't have a drinking problem, but I didn't have a drinking solution," he said.

By the time he was working in Europe, he needed a solution. He found it in Catholicism, though not in the Benedictine order for which his high school was named. Rather, Bannon removed alcohol from his life entirely by practicing the spiritual exercises conceived by St. Ignatius of Loyola, the founder of the Jesuit order.

Of the six books that are most important to him, three are religious, and, for Bannon, they form a trilogy. Ross Fuller's *The Brotherhood of the Common Life and Its Influence*, published in 1995, describes the formation of a medieval religious movement within the Catholic Church that is seen by some as a bridge to Protestantism. Gerard Groote (1340–1384), described by Ross as the founder and early "focal point" of the Brotherhood (or Brethren) of the Common Life, is a key figure for Bannon. Groote was, like Bannon, a voracious reader, but Groote came to believe it was more important to have the right knowledge than all knowledge. The Brethren emphasized the power of the layman to find God and live in religious communities (which the Brethren created) without taking permanent monastic vows. The early Brethren, Ross writes, were "feared by the establishment" and "the absence of vows invited accusations of heresy."[3] They advocated pursuit of the "mixed life" for the individual, devoting oneself to reflection and God but remaining rooted in this world.

The Brethren believed that laymen could find the path to God through daily meditation and prayer. Writing of another devotee of the "mixed life," Wessel Gansfort, Ross observes, "He is saying that God is approached more effectively with the help of an inward discipline of meditation and remembrance, discernment and love, which open the heritage of ritual and sacrifice, than through ordinary submission to the external framework of conventional discipline in such schools of Christianity as most monasteries had become."[4]

Through meditation on one's faith and life, one gained focus and self-knowledge, banishing disorder and idle thoughts. "In the morning and after the midday meal, establish before your eyes your bad habits, your chief weaknesses, and the virtues for which you are striving, and the way things were during the recent struggle with your enemies," wrote Gansforth. Groote and his followers believed such practices harkened to the customs of the early Christians and were necessary, as Groote wrote, "so that the heart may not be scattered in things."[5]

According to Ross, "The aim was given 'to gather together the soul.' Meditation was a means of utilizing the existing religious framework towards this aim...The gathering together of oneself through meditation was connected, for these religious men, with being more and more deeply 'in the presence of Jesus,' a proximity which, if real, cannot but influence the way a man acts."[6]

For Bannon, the practices of the Brethren are, in a general way, a means to "know thyself" and to better oneself in one's relationship with God. Also helpful to him in this regard is the classic devotional, *The Imitation of Christ*, widely regarded as the most influential Christian text next to the Bible. The work is attributed to *Thomas à Kempis* (1380–1471), a follower of Groote, but Bannon believes the work is actually Groote's and that à Kempis merely transcribed it. It counsels humility, separation from mundane cares of the world, and faith in Christ to obtain inner peace. "If I send you trouble and adversity, do not fret or let your heart be downcast," à Kempis writes in the voice of Christ. "I can raise you quickly up again and turn all your sorrow into joy."[7]

If the teachings of the Brethren and *The Imitation of Christ* offer a general framework for approaching meditation, *The Spiritual Exercises of Saint Ignatius of Loyola* (1491–1556), provide particulars and details. As originally written, the "spiritual exercises" are meant as a four-week retreat, though people use the exercises in various ways. Central to Ignatius's program is the "examen," a self-review of one's faith. "By this name of Spiritual Exercises is meant every way of examining one's conscience, of meditating, of contemplating, of praying vocally and mentally, and of performing other spiritual actions," Ignatius writes. "For as strolling, walking and running are bodily exercises, so every way of preparing and disposing the soul to rid itself of all the disordered tendencies, and, after it is rid, to seek and find the Divine Will as to the management of one's life for the salvation of the soul, is called a Spiritual Exercise."[8]

The book contains instructions for prayers and meditations to be followed each week, including this "Particular and Daily Examen" in the first week: "Immediately on rising...one ought to propose to guard himself with diligence against that particular sin or defect which he wants to correct and amend."[9]

When he was in the Navy, Bannon acquired a book called *Zen Catholicism*, and for a while he practiced Zen meditation and studied Eastern religions, even as he remained a Catholic. He initially used Eastern spirituality along with the exercises of St. Ignatius to defeat his drinking habit, but he eventually came to rely mainly on the Christian teachings. "I could center myself and get a practical program for each day," he said of St. Ignatius's exercises. "It's a five-step program to, essentially, become aware of the presence of God in your life, the presence of God as you review the day at the end of the day. You also then review the day with gratitude. You pay attention to what emotions you had at certain things. You choose, each day, what was the chief feature of that day—was that anger? Was it jealousy? It's just a way to settle yourself. To read religious texts in a certain way. Basically, you pray."

Bannon has done the "examen" every day since he stopped drinking, he says. He generally performs it in the morning and later reviews the day, through its perspective, at night. He has even done the full four-week program "probably ten times," though never in isolation at a retreat. "It's just a tool I've used," he said. "If I didn't have those tools available, I would not have been able to do it on my own. [With the help of a daily examen] I literally have never had the desire to have another drink. It gave me my life back. It's amazing."

Bannon looks back on his drinking days with some measure of contempt. Hanging out with the guys without a beer in his hand was a revelation. "First thing I noticed, fuck, these guys bore the shit out of me. It's all ridiculous," he said. "You sit there sober and you're sitting there going, 'I could not possibly have done this and thought it was great. Is this how I was?' I just noticed that, if you're not drinking it's the stupid hour."[10]

And Bannon didn't have time for stupid hours.

CHAPTER NINE

A Humane Economy

W hen Steve Bannon thinks about economics, he thinks about his dad. No one bailed out Marty Bannon when he lost most of his life savings in the 2008 financial crash. Steve Bannon still bears a grudge about that—about how middle-class and work-ing-class taxpayers got stuck with the bill from the self-serving financial and Washington establishment; he still inwardly fumes about a "free market" corrupted by corporatism and crony capital-ism; and he earnestly believes that the American economic miracle has more to do with the hard-working Marty Bannons of the world, and the values they hold, than it does with the current Me-Generation titans of Wall Street.

In early October 2008, the stock market was in a deep dive. Marty Bannon had been buying equity in his company, AT&T, all his life. He wanted to have something to leave to his children, and he borrowed against it when he needed to help his kids through college. "AT&T had a good offer on a stock employee plan, a few shares of stock by payroll deduction, and I worked hard to accumulate something decent through the years," Marty Bannon said. It was an investment in the company he'd worked for all his life, an investment in his family, and his faith in AT&T was firm. "That company and its stock, its equity, was only second to the Catholic Church in his constellation of what the ordered universe was about," Steve Bannon said.

Marty Bannon never made rash decisions. His family called him "Steady Eddie." But in the financial crisis of 2008, he had to make a fateful choice. With the stock market crashing, some analysts were advising investors to sell, to cut their losses, because things were only going to get worse. "I lost a sizable sum in value," Marty Bannon said. "I made the decision to sell some of it and that just kind of hits you hard."[1]

I was told repeatedly by people who know Steve Bannon well that Marty Bannon's financial loss was one of the most profound influences on Steve Bannon's thinking on economics and politics. In Steve Bannon's view, an irresponsible elite had ripped out a piece of his dad's soul and discarded it with casual disdain. "He basically sells the shares in the Catholic Church. He sells his shares in the ordered universe," Bannon said.

"All he is, is everyman," Steve said of his father. "He's the guy that put aside all of the joys of life—having the second or third car, having a vacation home, going traveling. He's just your standard, stock, great guy. Coaching Little League, doing all the stuff for the family and the church. He's the guy who holds civic society together—that is the backbone of the nation."

But, Bannon said, if you take out the backbone, the country collapses like Jell-O, because the elite aren't the ones who make everything work; they're not the ones who make the sacrifices that sustain the country. "There's a compact," Bannon said, with working-class and middle-class Americans, that might be unwritten but that is part of the American Dream. "If you do your stuff every day you're not going to get fucked. Your life's not going to be thrown away....All these people ask for is, 'Give me a stable economy that I can do my work and thrive in, and I'm not asking to be a millionaire—I don't want to be a millionaire, I just want to raise a family. And by the way, my sons and daughters will serve in the military. Just make sure it's in defense of the country—you're not throwing their lives away.'"[2]

Once, the elite were of the same mind about America as the working class. The elite upheld the culture and traditional American values, they were patriotic, they loved America and were willing to send their kids to fight and die for it if necessary, as, for example, Theodore Roosevelt did. "If you look at the leaders of capitalism at that time, when capitalism was, I believe, at its highest flower and spreading its benefits to most of mankind, almost all of those capitalists were strong believers in the Judeo-Christian West," Bannon said in remarks via Skype to a conference at the Vatican in 2014. "They were either active participants in the Jewish faith, they were active participants in the Christians' faith...and the underpinnings of their beliefs was manifested in the work they did."

Capitalism practiced in this manner generated "tremendous wealth," Bannon said. "And that wealth was really distributed among a middle class, a rising middle class, people who come from really working-class environments." No more. "I think that's incredibly important and something that would really become unmoored. I can see this on Wall Street today. I can see this with the securitization of everything...everything is looked at as a securitization opportunity. People are looked at as commodities. I don't believe that our forefathers had that same belief."[3]

The new establishment knows no party lines. It has no ethnic or religious boundaries (although most consider God irrelevant). It is centered on no particular occupation. The new establishment is united only in it selfishness and in its gaming of the system for its own financial privileges. "When you have this kind of crony capitalism, you have a different set of rules for the people that make the rules. It's this partnership of big government and corporatists," he told the conference at the Vatican.

Bannon added that the new elite practices "a form of capitalism that is taken away from the underlying spiritual and moral foundations of Christianity and, really, Judeo-Christian belief. It's something that should be at the heart of every Christian who is a capitalist—'What is the purpose of whatever I'm doing with this wealth? What is the purpose of what I'm doing with the ability that God has given us, that divine providence has given us to actually be a creator of jobs and a creator of wealth?'"

Bannon added, "The new form of capitalism is quite different when you really look at it to what I call the 'enlightened capitalism' of the Judeo-Christian West. It is a capitalism that really looks to make people commodities, and to objectify people, and to use them almost, as with many of the precepts of Marx. And that is a form of capitalism, particularly to a younger generation, [that] they're really finding quite attractive. And if they don't see another alternative, it's going to be an alternative that they gravitate to under this kind of rubric of 'personal freedom.'"

While the old elite recognized it benefited from and saw its success as advancing Western civilization, and felt some responsibility for society as a whole, the members of the new elite believe they have profited purely by their own merit. As they're the best and brightest, they have every right to remake the culture as they see fit—and to remake it without regard to

Judeo-Christian teaching or to European or American traditions that they consider irrelevant or to the values of those who didn't do as well—the bourgeois middle and working classes, the Marty Bannons of the world, or in Hillary Clinton's dismissive term, the "deplorables" who supported Donald Trump. On this point, Bannon has been deeply influenced by Christopher Lasch's 1995 book *The Revolt of the Elites and the Betrayal of Democracy.*

"Meritocracy is a parody of democracy," Lasch writes. "Social mobility does not undermine the influence of the elites; if anything it helps to solidify their influence by supporting the illusion that it rests solely on merit. It merely strengthens the likelihood that elites will exercise power irresponsibly, precisely because they recognize so few obligations to their predecessors or to the communities they profess to lead. Their lack of gratitude disqualifies meritocratic elites from the burden of leadership, and in any case, they are less interested in leadership than in escaping from the common lot—the very definition of meritocratic success."

He continues:

> Although hereditary advantages play an important part in the attainment of professional or managerial status, the new class has to maintain the fiction that its power rests on intelligence alone. Hence it has little sense of ancestral gratitude or an obligation to live up to responsibilities inherited from the past. It thinks of itself as a self-made elite owing its privileges exclusively to its own efforts....Populated by transients, they lack the continuity that derives from a sense of place and from standards of conduct self-consciously cultivated and handed down from generation to generation.

Simultaneously arrogant and insecure, the new elites, the professional classes in particular, regard the masses with mingled scorn and apprehension....Their snobbery lacks any acknowledgment of reciprocal obligations between the favored few and the multitude.[4]

Lasch argues that today it is the middle class and the working class who are the final stewards of a great culture threatened with disintegration, and who understand there are limits to the grand schemes of the "meritocrats." Middle America maintains instincts that are "demonstrably more conservative than those of their self-appointed spokesmen and would-be liberators," Lasch writes. "It is the working and lower middle classes, after all, that favor limits on abortion, cling to the two-parent family as a source of stability in a turbulent world, resist experiments with 'alternative lifestyles,' and harbor deep reservations about affirmative action and other ventures in large-scale social engineering."[5]

Diminishing the middle class presents a danger to all, rich and poor. "The decline of nations is closely linked, in turn, to the global decline of the middle class. Ever since the 16th and 17th centuries the fortunes of the nation state have been bound up with those of the trading and manufacturing classes....The middle class under-standably became the most patriotic, not to say jingoistic and militaristic element in society. But the unattractive features of middle-class nationalism should not obscure its positive contribu-tions in the form of a highly developed sense of place in respect for historical continuity—hallmarks of the middle-class sensibility that can be appreciated more fully now that middle-class culture is everywhere in retreat. Whatever its faults, middle-class nationalism provided a common ground, common standards, a common frame of reference without which society dissolves into nothing more than contending factions, as the founding fathers of America understood so well—a war of all against all."

Lasch condemns what Bannon would call "the Party of Davos," a reference to the Swiss Alpine city where the world's economic elite gather every year to figure out what's best for mankind. "The market in which the new elites operate is now international in scope. Their fortunes are tied to enterprises that operate across boundaries," Lasch writes. "They are more concerned with the smooth functioning of the system as a whole than with any of its parts. Their loyalties—if the term is not itself anachronistic in this context—are international rather than regional, national, or local. They have more in common with their counterparts in Brussels or Hong Kong than with the masses of Americans not yet plugged into the network of global communications."

Bannon notes that he's worked closely with the elite in business, finance, Hollywood, and the military—from California to Washington to New York to London and Paris. "I can tell you, they ain't that smart," he said. "I say this all the time. It's a riff on Buckley. If you give me the choice of being governed by the first 100 people that show up at a Tea Party rally—the choice of the first fucking hundred people that walk through that door in a Donald Trump rally—or the top 100 partners at Goldman Sachs, I will take the 100 people that walk into those rallies every day and we'll have a better, more equitable, more fairly managed country. Because you know why? They're the backbone of the country, and they kind of get it." It's not, he told me, that people like those at Goldman Sachs are bad people. "They just live in this kind of globalist reality, the party of Davos, where what happens in Shanghai and what happens in Chelsea, and London, and what happens in Paris or the Hamptons is more what drives them than what happens" among average Americans.[6]

"Brexit," the British referendum vote in favor of separating from the European Union, the victory of Trump, and the shockingly strong challenge by Bernie Sanders against Hillary Clinton in 2016, all demonstrate to Bannon that populism is a rising force and the future for both the Democrats and Republicans.

"Populist nationalism is the winner," Bannon says. "Now it is on the right side of history." The question is whether the leftist or the conservative iteration of it will triumph. "The only debate going forward will be [whether] it'll be British Labor leader Jeremy Corbyn's and Bernie Sanders's views of populism or Donald Trump's view and Indian [Prime Minister] Modi's view of populism. Whether it will be a culturally right and economically conservative [populism] or whether it will be socialistic and more."

Bannon says that today's populism is "a global rejection of the man in the street to the Party of Davos. And here's why. The party of Davos has tried to put in a cookie-cutter solution. Their template for how the world should be. It should be built upon a neoliberal model throughout the world. Guess what? That may not work."[7]

The "Party of Davos," which includes the elite of both parties, bankrupted itself, both morally and literally, Bannon argues, with the 2008 financial crash. "All the experts, the Party of Davos," brought our financial system, Bannon said, to "complete, total, abject failure. I don't need to hear from these people anymore. It took $1 trillion, and guess what? [It's] paid for by the Marty Bannons of the world, and not one guy goes to jail later. Zero accountability. In fact, they all made tons of money because of the infusion of cash by the taxpayer, by the little guy. The party of Davos—when it's all going right they get all the upside and the little guy gets nothing. He gets more foreign competition. He gets illegal aliens." And he gets competition from guys with "H1-B visas."

"When things go wrong," Bannon added, the Party of Davos doesn't suffer, they just "get the taxpayer to pay for it. So the little guy making $55,000—where is his stock? Where's his bailout?"[8]

The working men and women of the world "are just tired of being dictated to by what we call the party of Davos," Bannon said in his remarks to the Vatican. They know best for themselves "about how to raise their families and how to educate their families. So I think you're seeing a global reaction to centralized government, whether that government is in Beijing or that government is in Washington, DC, or that government is in Brussels."

"It's incumbent upon freedom-loving people to make sure that we sort out these governments and make sure that we sort out particularly this crony capitalism so that the benefits become more of this entrepreneurial spirit and that can flow back to working-class and middle-class people," Bannon said.[9]

★

Part of this economic vision of Bannon's comes from his reading of American history, and his understanding of the economic model that America followed well into the twentieth century. This economic model was called "the American System" or, alternatively, "Hamiltonianism."

And for Bannon, one of the crucial parts of the American system is maintaining a manufacturing base—not just for its economic benefits, but for its cultural ones, linking work and profit with tangible goods. In his movie *Generation Zero*, a narrator warns that, "For a culture to believe that it can be a consumer-based society that doesn't produce, that can shift wealth around, that isn't commonly grounded in a firm moral fiber," is to risk events like the 2008 financial crash.

Bannon's natural sympathies are with the worker, not the capitalist—though he's been a pretty good capitalist himself. "He's always been, ever since I can remember, the person for the little guy," said his sister Mary Beth. "Even as a little sister he would always defend me, even if like an older brother was picking on me, he would always step in and defend me. It's just in his nature."[10]

The American System essentially looked out for the little guy. It supported an economy that put American workers front and center. It has been replaced, however, by an ever-growing, neoliberal emphasis on free trade, which Bannon believes has resulted in grievous damage to the culture and the middle class. "Our problem in the United States is quite simple," Bannon told me. "We have deindustrialized this country and sent all the good jobs to China, India, and Brazil. That's the problem. We've shipped them all overseas. We've been gamed. This thing called free trade? We've been gamed by the mercantilist policy of China, India, and Brazil. And so there are no jobs," he said. "China is exporting at both deflation and overcapacity."

Bannon believes that we can slash the welfare rolls—and Republicans can win minority voters—by regaining blue-collar jobs that have been exported overseas. "The reason why I think people are looking for a paternalistic, you know, government entitlement program is the fact that we gutted all the good jobs in this country," he said. "And it's going to be a very tough, very nasty fight to get those jobs back. China, Brazil, and India are just not going to turn around and say, 'Fine let's export them all back to the United States.'"[11]

For much of American history, essentially through World War II, the United States followed what today might be dismissed as a "protectionist" trade program, starting with America's two most distinguished protectionists, George Washington and Alexander

Hamilton. Under the American System, the United States sought to protect its industries from overseas competition, particularly when it came to manufacturing.

Moreover, protectionism was Republican orthodoxy. It was Democrats, especially Southern Democrats, who wanted free trade, so that they could better export cotton and other agricultural products, and import lower cost (if there were lower tariffs) foreign manufactured goods. Abraham Lincoln, the first Republican president, signed two tariff bills during the Civil War, and protectionism remained standard Republican policy through Herbert Hoover.

"The administration of Abraham Lincoln inaugurated an era that lasted until World War II, in which the United States had the most protected home market in the world," Michael Lind, an author much admired by Bannon, wrote in his economic history of the United States. "Between 1867 and 1914, while many goods were admitted free from duties, the U.S. tariff on dutiable imports, chiefly manufactured goods, hovered between 40 and 50 percent."[12] In fact, before the first non-wartime income tax became law in 1913, the federal government was largely financed by tariffs. Lind and Bannon say it's a myth that the Smoot-Hawley Tariff Act of 1930 either caused or worsened the depression.

"American economic nationalism is the birthright of, intellectually, not just conservatives, but the nation—from Alexander Hamilton to Jackson, Clay, Polk, Lincoln, all the way up to Teddy Roosevelt," Bannon said. "The American System is laid out by Henry Clay. And by the way, they said that the most radical idea, as bad as anything that came out of the French Revolution, was free trade. The American System—the first Trump guys were Hamilton, Jackson, Clay, Polk, Lincoln, and Roosevelt. A group of people that believed in American economic nationalism."[13]

As America's first Treasury secretary, Hamilton was entrusted with the task of putting the fledgling independent U.S. economy on a strong footing. Hamilton perceived that the United States would come out on the losing end long-term if it adopted the *laissez-faire* "British System" of economics. Since Britain was the manufacturing giant of the age, America would not be able to develop its own industries if it didn't protect its emerging businesses from British imports. When it came to protection, Hamilton favored direct subsidies for U.S. manufacturers more than tariffs, and he thought the issue was not just one of economics but of sovereignty.

"Alexander Hamilton and our other founding fathers understood that any nation that desires to remain politically independent must also protect its economic independence and strive toward as much self-sufficiency as possible," wrote author William J. Gill. "The whole concept of nationhood rests upon this premise. Only those nations which intend to eventually surrender their sovereignty completely will abandon protectionism and trade to the extent that the United States has done in recent decades."[14]

Senator Henry Clay, the leading proponent of the American System in the early and mid-nineteenth century, advocated tariffs to help America gain "the immense power of machinery" for itself. Washington, Hamilton, and Clay saw a domestic manufacturing base as a critical element of U.S. national security. Hamilton and Clay backed federal support for infrastructure development, which was initially used for roads and canals and then accelerated under Lincoln with the allocation of millions of dollars for the Pacific rail line.[15]

"In the middle of fighting a war for the very soul of this country, [Lincoln's] focus, legislatively, was on the Homestead Act," which granted land out West to settlers, "and the transcontinental railroad," Bannon said.

Bannon believes the American System needs to be reinstated. America still needs a manufacturing base for all the reasons that Washington, Hamilton, Clay, Lincoln, and Theodore Roosevelt knew, and for all the new challenges that they would understand: to support the working class, to reduce the income gap between rich and poor, to ensure our national security, and to perpetuate traditional American culture. "The American System is the center-piece," Bannon said. "A country is not an economy. A country is a culture that has an economy. The American System is about the nurturing of an economy that has manufacturing, agriculture—all of that—that can sustain the American family, and therefore, American society."[16]

In Bannon's view, the loss of manufacturing has damaged one of our country's classic, vaunted features, American ingenuity. "It's one of the reasons we don't innovate as much—all the factories are gone," Bannon said. American factories, staffed by skilled, practi-cal laborers, could test new, constructive ideas immediately. It was American ingenuity, the ingenuity of the American working man, not financial trades on Wall Street, that built this country, Bannon told me, and that are ultimately "the guarantor of our security, our sovereignty, our freedom."

To Bannon, the economists, with their cost-benefit analyses on free trade, are missing the point. "The return on equity, return on investment, is not the thing that is the highest thing in the church of America. It's not," Bannon told me. But if you say otherwise, particularly among Republican elites, "You are literally at that point, a heathen."

"You know the thing that turned me off and reinforced my belief in the working people" was reading Ayn Rand and her libertarian philosophy of Objectivism. "I think Ayn Rand is one of the most dangerous individuals in modern thought." He granted that he shares some libertarian views, but that "Her idea of, there's this leadership class that is so elite, it all depends upon them, and their well-being and their nurturing....It's just something I totally disagree with. I think it's against human nature, and certainly against all the precepts of the Judeo-Christian West." Bannon doubts "that capitalism was just supposed to be about the allocation of resources." He believes it is undergirded by deeper values, arising from the Christian culture in which it grew. And in America it was guided by the values of the American System. Bannon argues that once you break that culture, once you lose those values, you risk losing everything. "Look at America in 2017. We're so close to losing America as the culture we know," Bannon lamented. "That's why there's an opioid crisis. I mean, we have a crisis in the Midwest and with the working-class around the country where people have lost their jobs, and now they have to get government assistance. They lose their dignity. And what do they do? They do opioids and go look at pornography." But the economy can still be saved from the "radical capitalists" who advocate free trade. "There is nothing about free-trade or what these radical capitalists are talking about that is holy writ," he said. "It's not physics. It can be changed by the agency of man."[17]

★

Bannon suggests the country's greatest exports today are its own industries. "We're a colony" of China, he says. "We are Jamestown to their Great Britain. We ship them copper, and we ship them oil and natural gas, and beef, and agricultural products. Yes, we do ship some Boeing jets and some other things, but essentially, we're a colony of theirs."

Bannon argues that America is also being colonized through immigration—de facto open borders—that he considers a cultural suicide pact, given foolish and short-sighted justification by some conservatives on economic grounds.

In 2014, on a trip to visit the Breitbart Texas bureau that was just getting started, Bannon went to the Mexican border. The experience rattled him. He noticed not only that illegal immigrants were pouring into the United States, but that the *Texas* side of the border was terrorized by Mexican drug cartels. "The Mexican border really starts 40 miles into Texas," he told me in 2017. And illegal aliens were "just coming across the border, it's just open." Back in Dallas, he asked a local official how this could be.

"What's going on? The state is run by Republicans."

"Oh, it's because the guys that finance the Republican Party want it," the official responded.

"What do you mean?" asked Bannon, incredulous.

"Well, the big guys who do it are the building construction guys. That's all illegal alien labor. The oil guys, it's all illegal, and agriculture, that's all illegal too."

"Are you kidding me?"

The official assured him it was all true. "Oh yeah. Everybody knows that."

Bannon felt like an idiot. "It started crystalizing my thinking that the elites get the joke, right?" he said. They get cheap labor and higher profits and the little guy maybe loses his job, his neighborhood crime rate goes up, and he almost certainly starts losing his culture, which matters to him more than it does to the elites. "It's the little guy that has no representation. It is not that we don't know what the problems of the country are," he said. The issue is that the politicians serve the interests of the elite, not the American middle class and working class.[18]

The low-skill, low-wage, non-English speaking people entering the United States from Mexico are taking jobs from Americans,

Bannon strongly believes. "The people most affected by illegal, alien labor, is the black working class and the Hispanic working class," he said. "Go into the inner city. That's why they're not paying a guy 12 bucks or 13 bucks to flip burgers at McDonald's. Because they don't have to! They get all the labor they want."

Bannon seeks not just to end illegal immigration, but he wants to vastly curb legal immigration and reduce the number of refugees the United States takes. "Until we have the black working class and the Hispanic working class getting high-value-added jobs, we've failed as a society. To me: citizens first. And we don't need a million immigrants in this country. Particularly, we don't need a million immigrants that don't come with a real set of skills."

The problem even trickles up to the ease with which better-educated immigrants can enter the country, he says. They, Bannon says, are crowding out American black and Hispanic students from getting advanced degrees. Foreign students, Bannon noted, will pay much more for graduate schools because they're subsidized by their home governments, while American citizens, subsidized by the schools themselves with financial aid, may pay far less, which makes it more profitable for universities to accept foreign students. "The population of blacks and Hispanics in graduate schools, in engineering, is virtually nil. We can't sustain ourselves in that," he said. "We can't change an entire elementary school program in this country to STEM—science, technology, engineering, and math—and then not have a natural place for these kids to go to school and to have jobs."

But the influx of immigrants is about more than jobs for Bannon. It has to do with whether America's culture can survive. "Civic society" doesn't work when American citizens keep looking over their shoulder worried that their jobs might be sent overseas or that they might be replaced by cheaper immigrant labor. An

American citizen can even feel like a second-class citizen in his own country when the elites tell him that "we're not gonna allow the world to come in and compete with you on a daily basis for your freaking job," Bannon said. "The direction of your life is to build civic society. What we want those guys doing is coaching little leagues, building churches, and being there for that kind of social interconnectivity that makes America so special, right? And raising happy, healthy families." But how do they do that when they're not only fearful for their jobs, but the culture around them is changing so dramatically?

Bannon says, "We're a nation of *citizens*; we're not a nation of immigrants," correcting what he believes is a common misperception. "So now we have to start to act like citizens come first. All policy should be oriented to making the working people in this country and the middle class in this country have a better shot at success. And we've gotten away from that. What we've done is brought in huge global competition for their jobs, for their schools."[19]

Bannon, on his Breitbart radio show, interviewed Trump on November 19, 2015. At the time, Trump was more liberal on immigration than Bannon was, making the case that the United States should try to keep talented foreign-born students.

"When somebody is going to Harvard, Yale, Princeton, Penn, Stanford, all the greats, and they graduate, and not only graduate, but do great, and we throw them out of the country, and they can't get back in, I think that's terrible. We've got to be able to keep great people in the country." Trump said. "We have to be careful of that, Steve. You know, we have to keep our talented people in this country."

Bannon: "Um."

Trump: "I think you agree with that. Do you agree with that?"

Bannon did not. "A country's more than an economy," he said. "We're a civic society."[20]

★

For Bannon, American culture is a very specific thing that can be corrupted and destroyed. "It's the things we've been passed from time immemorial. The Judeo-Christian culture that we have," he said. "I'm not a multiculturalist." America has "an underlying culture, that has been passed down from Jerusalem, to Athens, to Rome, to London. It's the belief in self-reliance, it's the belief in the self-determination of the individual. It's freedom to be the traditional family. The culture that is our way of life. I think it's absolutely vital and important. And we have an obligation to those that came before us as much as we have an obligation to the people in the future to pass that down."[21]

One of the six books Bannon listed as most important to him was Edward Gibbon's eighteenth-century masterpiece, *The History of the Decline and Fall of the Roman Empire*. Bannon loves it for Gibbon's use of language. "The language is so powerful, it's so well written, it just gets you to understand the English language and the power of the language." But much more than that, he believes it is the best history of the "people most like us," the Romans. The book charts how "They built this great empire and how it all slipped away over time." Bannon sees Rome's decline and fall as centering primarily on two factors: the elite class became corrupt and detached from the citizenry and the empire became overrun by immigrants, or the people we know as the "barbarians." At first, Bannon said of the incorporation of barbarians into the empire, "it worked perfectly," just as the melting pot in America used to work. "You can see that power of Roman virtue, these

Roman virtues of manliness, and service to the state. And that's why everybody in the world wanted a part of that."

But the "concentration of wealth" at the top corrupted the elite. "The elites quit serving in the military, they became so enormously wealthy versus everyone else, who became essentially indentured servants," he said. The elite "became detached," they became, at least to themselves, "god-like," which is how today's elite "in Silicon Valley and Wall Street, the super billionaires" think of themselves—masters of the universe. The Roman elite "became detached from what the state is really about…its citizens. And you could see that they were not prepared to take the onslaught of these massive migrations that continued to crush them in the 400s."

The Roman Senate "was bought and paid for by the elites.… The exact thing we face today!" he exclaimed. "What the Roman Empire faced is exactly what we face, that you lose the citizenship—and the power of citizenship—of the Roman Republic, you become an Empire, and that empire becomes a massive concentration of power and wealth, which is detached from the people. And then eventually, you're having people who don't want to serve in the legions, you have to go for foreign soldiers. Everybody is a mercenary. And therefore, no one really stood up or was prepared to die, really, in service to the country. And then what happened? Wave, after wave, after wave of migrations from the Goths, the Visigoths, the Huns. Coming into the empire and changing the culture and destroying the civic society they had in Rome. The empire could not withstand it."

"It's a lesson for today," he said. "These massive migrations of people destroyed the basic culture."[22]

For Bannon, economics and immigration form a single subject—and that subject is cultural and raises the question of what makes for a humane economy and a sustainable state. His argument is that

America's future lies in the wise policies of its past—the American System of protection, including the promotion of American culture and the values of citizenship, and today, the protection of our borders as well.

CHAPTER TEN

Defending the West

Bannon often thinks in military terms and—given his unquenchable interest in history—he thinks of America's foreign policy challenges in world historical terms.

Nowhere is this truer than in America's battle with radical Islamic terror. For Bannon, the war on terror did not begin on September 11, 2001. He sees this war as part of a long history of conflict between Christendom and the Muslim world. In conversation, he casually reels off the Battle of Tours in 732 between the Franks and the Umayyad Caliphate, *The Song of Roland*, which describes Charlemagne fighting Muslims in Spain in 778, the Battle of Lepanto in 1571 between the Holy League and the Ottoman Empire, and the Battle of Vienna fought between Catholic armies and the Ottomans in 1683. "So, it's been a struggle for a long time, and you see it playing out today in the modern world," he said. "If you look back at the long history of the Judeo-Christian

West's struggle against Islam, I believe that our forefathers kept their stance, and I think they did the right thing. I think they kept it out of their world, whether it was at Vienna, or Tours, or other places," he told the conference at the Vatican. "It bequeathed to us the great institution that is the Church of the West."[1]

Bannon pinpointed 1979 as a key year in the latest round of conflict between the West and the Muslim world. It was the year the Soviets invaded Afghanistan; the year the Ayatollah Khomeini seized power in Iran; and, what he says is the most important and overlooked event, the year that Muslim extremists occupied the Grand Mosque in Mecca for two weeks, declared the Mahdi, or the "redeemer," had arrived, and called for the overthrow of the House of Saud. After the Saudi military cleared out the militants in a bloody battle, the Saudis decided to appease and grant more power to Wahhabi mullahs who preach an aggressive and extreme form of Islam. "It's the most fundamental thing in our modern history which nobody talks about. And the reason they don't talk about it is the Saudis and other people don't want to talk about it," Bannon asserted. "As the Puritans were to Protestantism or Catholicism, so the Wahhabis and the Salafis are to Islam," Bannon said. "And that austere version has metastasized to be this threat of radical Islamic terror which now is stalking Western Europe, and it's driving many of the problems in the world today."[2]

But Bannon emphasizes, "We're not enemies of Islam," which he calls, "a major, great religion in the world." We are enemies of the Islamists who preach a political Islam, a universal Islamic empire, and a Sharia Law that supersedes all else, including the laws of the countries where they live. "As the Judeo-Christian West, we stand absolutely opposed to the precepts and the tenets of radical Islamic terror," he said. "To the degree that that continues to purport an Islamic supremacy, it's just not going to work. I mean, we have to face a very brutal fact that, if you're an Islamic supremacist, if you believe in the supremacy of Islam over all the forms of worship…it has to affect the way people conduct and comport themselves in their daily lives."

Bannon calls militant Islam "theocratic" and says that it "imposes" itself on "civil society." He adds, "The West stands absolutely opposed to that. Whether that is in Jerusalem, whether that is in St. Petersburg, whether that is in London, or whether that is in Washington, DC. We are absolutely opposed to that as a culture. And if that is what this war is going to be about, then so be it."

Mosques and Muslim schools in the West that preach sedition must be confronted. "If it can be shown that some of these schools, some of these mosques, some of these Islamic centers, are teaching, particularly, Islamic supremacy, then I think that's a problem. I think it has to be addressed a lot more aggressively," he said.

"I think you're seeing in Islam right now, I think you're seeing their Thirty Years' War," Bannon said. "I think you're seeing the civil war in Islam, between Shiite and Sunni, but most importantly, I think between the radical adherents of an austere, puritanical aspect of it, against the more moderate Islam, that's kind of going through a realignment." There are those within the Islamic world who back reform within Islam, "more moderate voices…that are telling their own people: this has to change." He adds, "It will work itself out."

The Obama administration sometimes appeared to give preference to radical groups, like the Muslim Brotherhood. But reforming moderates like Egyptian President Abdel Fattah el-Sisi (who took power in a coup against President Mohamed Morsi of the Muslim Brotherhood), are, in Bannon's view, America's allies in this struggle. In January 2015, President el-Sisi said, with admirable frankness to a gathering of Muslim leaders, "We are in need of a religious revolution....The entire world is waiting on you. The entire world is waiting for your word...because the Islamic world is being torn, it is being destroyed, it is being lost. And it is being lost by our own hands."

El-Sisi, himself a practicing Muslim, continued, "It's inconceivable that the thinking that we hold most sacred should cause the entire Islamic world to be a source of anxiety, danger, killing and destruction for the rest of the world. Impossible that this thinking—and I am not saying the religion—I am saying this thinking... is antagonizing the entire world. It's antagonizing the entire world! Does this mean that 1.6 billion [Muslims] should want to kill the rest of the world's inhabitants—that is 7 billion—so that they themselves may live? Impossible!"[3]

Bannon notes that while any religion can become radicalized or have radical elements, radicalism has been, and is, more prevalent and dangerous within Islam. "You don't see" the same sort of "enforcement of radical forms of Christianity," he says; and indeed, if anything, the West's Christian faith has become so attenuated that the West might have neither the insight nor the will that it previously had to fight radical Islam.[4]

In his 2014 remarks at the Vatican, Bannon said of radical Islam, "The secular West is not prepared to handle it. I think there's a major crisis in Christianity today. Western Europe is not going to church. All these great cathedrals and churches are being abandoned as the West loses its actual practicing part of Christianity."

He continued, "I believe the world, and particularly the Judeo-Christian West, is in a crisis," he said. "The immense secularization" of the West is weakening it. "If you look at younger people, especially millennials under 30, the overwhelming drive of popular culture is to absolutely secularize this rising" generation; that generation has been stripped of the historical understanding and religious conviction that would prepare it to fight the Islamist establishment of a new Caliphate.

"We are in an outright war against jihadist Islamic fascism. And this war is, I think, metastasizing far quicker than governments can handle it," he told his Vatican audience. "We're at the very beginning stages of a very brutal and bloody conflict, of which, if the people in this room, the people in the church, do not bind together and really form what I feel is an aspect of the church militant, to really be able to not just stand with our beliefs, but to fight for our beliefs against this new barbarity that's starting, that will completely eradicate everything that we've been bequeathed over the last 2,000, 2,500 years," he said. When the democracies fought Germany, Italy, and Japan, they were strengthened with a greater sense of their culture and religion. The current crisis in Judeo-Christian culture undermines not only the will to fight but the success of the capitalist system that built the war machine that defeated the fascists. It was "really the Judeo-Christian West versus atheists, right?" he said of World War II. "The underlying principle is an enlightened form of capitalism, that capitalism really gave us the wherewithal. It kind of organized and built the materials needed to support, whether it's the Soviet Union, England, the United States, and eventually to take back continental Europe and to beat back a barbaric empire in the Far East."[5]

The calls for tolerance that come after every Islamist outrage are, to Bannon, the infantile responses of a shallow, secularized people who do not understand the full dimensions of the threat. "Look at what happens in Manchester and London. The same thing. You had these brutal killings, and then automatically you have the flowers, and you have the crying, and you have the same response every time." Tougher medicine is needed, including slashing the number of Muslim refugees permitted to enter the West.

"Why are we even letting the people over here that we're monitoring, that are costing us hundreds of billions of dollars? We have to clean this up. And it has to be cleaned up in short order or we're just asking for more and more trouble."[6]

★

Torchbearer, Bannon's 2016 documentary featuring *Duck Dynasty*'s Phil Robertson, highlights the current weakness of the West by describing the danger that presents itself when societies turn from God. Not only do they become weak when confronted with peril from without, but they face degradation from within. Without religion, the film asserts, man's law reigns, not God's, and while God's values are both good and eternal, man on his own will make it up as he goes along, with potentially grave consequences.

"Divorced from God the city of man devolves into strife, war, and the will to power over others," Robertson says. "Which eventually ends in ruin." Robertson notes that America's Founding Fathers assumed man's rights were "endowed by their Creator." Therefore, they cannot be taken away by the government or other men. "What anchor do you have for human dignity and rights once you forget where your rights come from? When men begin to determine what's right and what's wrong?" Robertson asks. "Oh my goodness," he answers, and the documentary then turns to the bloody, atheistic French Revolution. It moves on to the twentieth century and the atheist Nazis and takes the viewer to both the Auschwitz and Birkenau death camps.

The film condemns as false gods "hyper-rationalism," the "worship of science," and subjective morality, all of which lead to the death camps or to revolutionary terror. Robertson asks: "If you live by the utilitarian belief in the greatest good for the greatest number of people, what happens when the majority decides it's in your own good to kill all the Jews?"

The film continues with footage of Martin Luther King Jr. and the civil rights movement, an obvious example of a minority with God's moral law on their side fighting the oppression of the majority. Ironically, for someone who routinely gets accused by the most strident voices of being a Nazi, two of the most significant segments in this, Bannon's most recent film, concern the civil rights movement as a moral cause and the Holocaust as the result of an immoral ideology.

The documentary describes the moral degradation within our own society driven by a rejection of God. "We'll all be dead soon so who cares? Live for yourself. You decide right and wrong," is the thinking, Robertson says. "We are no longer image bearers" of God, "we are crotch-driven animals following our instincts," he intones, as we are shown scenes from debauched popular entertainment.

The film then contrasts graphic scenes of Islamist terrorists killing people, with Robertson baptizing people, a not so subtle reminder that while Islamists love death, conservative Christians like Robertson love life. Bannon believes the West needs to revive the Judeo-Christian belief and traditions that made it great and that will defend it during its current struggle against radical Islam.

But that struggle, he is quick to point out, does not mean endless war for the United States against extremists from a global religion. Prudence needs to be as much a part of American strategy as will and military might, and while America can encourage and support moderate Muslims, there is no need for America to intervene all over the Muslim world; America has its own national interests to pursue that supersede the civil war within Islam.

Bannon is cautious about military adventures in general and ardently opposed to putting American troops in harm's way unless it is absolutely necessary. For Bannon, it's always "America First." He rejects "nation-building" as unworkable; thinks that rather than trying to democratize the world, we should pursue our national interests; and believes that trying to mold other countries in our own democratic image is a fool's errand. Bannon would dispute the notion that America is "an idea" rather than a country. America's culture is based on a particular history shaped by particular people coming from a particular tradition. We are an outpost of the Judeo-Christian, English-speaking West. Other countries have far different traditions and need to find their own way. The conservative tradition in the West is based on our biblical heritage, an understanding that man is imperfect, and a distrust of utopian schemes such as global democracy as promoted by liberals and neo-conservatives. "We are *not* utopians. We understand the fallibility of man. The people grounded in the Jewish faith know this probably better than anybody," he told me. In the Old Testament God is often angry at his "chosen people," who receive God's word, and yet stray from it. "And then Christianity, which is nothing more than an offshoot of Judaism, is even more of that. It talks about the fallibility of man. Because we are a branch of Judaism, we believe in original sin. Original sin says that man is imperfect.... As conservatives...we don't believe in utopia."

Liberals, however, do think man is perfectible and think bureaucrats and government can get us there, and that history and tradition are irrelevant. Bannon strongly disagrees. "If you look at what happened when the Berlin Wall came down, Clinton and the Party of Davos, the 'great thinkers' around Clinton, immediately tried to force upon the Russian people this democratic model," he said. "And if you opposed that, people say 'Oh, you're anti-Democratic, you want totalitarianism.' No. I have respect for how societies come along over long periods of time and how people kind of know how to manage their lives at their own local level." And they will come to our way of thinking "when they're ready to come to it."[7]

Bannon is a great student of Thucydides' *History of the Peloponnesian War*, which, for him, provides signal lessons against an interventionist foreign policy. He makes particular note of the hubris of the Athenian elite who thought they could defeat both Sparta and Syracuse (the latter in an ill-fated expedition to defend Athenian allies) and met nemesis and defeat.

"If you think about it, one thing you have to remember is the law of unintended consequences," Bannon said. "That's what Thucydides teaches. It's just very powerful. All leaders should read it. You just see the frustrations. You see the mistakes made, you see good men trying to do the right thing for their cause. All the failures, and the successes. But principally the failures." Athens had spread itself too thin and gotten involved in an unnecessary conflict that cost it dearly. Thucydides also showed how difficult it could be for a democracy, Athens, to take on a dictatorship, Sparta, in war. "A totalitarian government has a certain mindset, and it's a command government. It's like Russia in the Second World War," he said. "They can lose 40 million people because they don't have to stand for elections." In a democracy, "you gotta be focused when you're doing these kinds of things, that you do it in a smart way."[8]

After Trump's election, Bannon gave colleagues copies of David Halberstam's *The Best and the Brightest*, a book he had plowed through many times and that is another great warning against hubris. It describes how the Washington elite of the Democratic Party dragged America into the quagmire of Vietnam. "*The Best and the Brightest* is nothing but a chapter of Thucydides," Bannon told me. "What Halberstam gets through [to the reader] is that the best and the brightest didn't have a lot of character, they didn't really understand the lessons of what Indochina was saying, what the people were saying," he said. "And they didn't have the quality of character to drop the arrogance, this Western arrogance, this elitism, that, 'I know everything, I'm the smartest guy.'"

Bannon believes the Washington elite, the liberals and the neo-conservatives, still have not learned the lessons of Thucydides or Halberstam. "So between the Iraq war and [Afghanistan], what has the little guy got to show for it? The lives of his sons and daughters completely thrown away. Let's be brutally frank. Their lives in Afghanistan and Iraq were just thrown away. All the injuries and all the trillion dollars in net present value, they were thrown away. Because people didn't know what they were doing. Or lied about it or had other things in mind than the defense of the country."

Plutarch's *Lives of the Noble Greeks and Romans*, another of Bannon's top six books, teaches the virtues that politicians must have to lead wisely and avoid military catastrophes. "Anybody who wants to get in politics or to know about power and know about, not just military action, but how men react in situations, has to read *Plutarch's Lives*," Bannon said. "What Plutarch does is take a Greek and a Roman. He writes a biography of one and then writes the biography of the other, and then he compares and contrasts. He has an analysis. That's the power of it. The analysis is how Greek society was, how Roman society was, and then the analysis of the character of both" biographical subjects. With America as the new Rome, Bannon finds Greco-Roman history endlessly instructive, and thinks it is folly not to benefit from the lessons of history.[9]

★

But if Gibbon and Plutarch and Thucydides are famous historians that most educated people are at least somewhat familiar with, Bannon's incessant and eclectic reading has also brought him to writers of a more esoteric and controversial bent.

In February 2017, the *New York Times* picked up on a mention Bannon had made in his remarks to the Vatican of Italian philosopher Julius Evola, a thinker admired by fascists—like Benito Mussolini. "But for all the examination of those remarks, a passing reference by Mr. Bannon to an esoteric Italian philosopher has gone little noticed, except perhaps by scholars and followers of the deeply taboo, Nazi-affiliated thinker, Julius Evola," the *Times* reported.

The discovery of Bannon's mention of Evola sparked a minor uproar. Bannon did indeed refer to Evola, but his intention was not to endorse Evola's support for fascism but to highlight Evola's writings on the power of traditionalism and the modern world's destruction of national cultures. Bannon spoke of Evola in the context of Vladimir Putin's popularity in Russia. "Vladimir Putin, when you really look at some of the underpinnings of some of his beliefs today, a lot of those come from what I call Eurasianism," Bannon said. "He's got an adviser who harkens back to Julius Evola and different writers of the early 20th century who are really the supporters of what's called the traditionalist movement, which really eventually metastasized into Italian fascism. A lot of people that are traditionalists are attracted to that. One of the reasons is that they believe that at least Putin is standing up for traditional institutions, and he's trying to do it in a form of nationalism," Bannon continued. "I think that people, particularly in certain countries, want to see sovereignty for their country, they want to see nationalism for their country. They don't believe in this kind of pan-European Union," he said.

He added that while he was not "justifying Vladimir Putin" and Putin's "kleptocracy," the "Judeo-Christian West" might learn something from the Russian leader's respect for traditionalism and his nationalism. "I happen to think that the individual sovereignty of a country is a good thing and a strong thing," Bannon said.[10]

Bannon told me he well understands the evil aspects of Evola. "He's not a great guy," Bannon said. "I'm not arguing he's a great guy." But Bannon says Evola and another philosopher with similar views, René Guénon, a French thinker who converted to Islam, both stress timeless, transcendent, and substantive values that are critical both to individuals and nations. "They argue that the modern world is becoming thinner. Its experiences are becoming thinner because it's taking out the transcendent." Medieval life lacked modern appliances and is mocked today, but "the guys would go on the field and they would pray five times a day. The simple peasants, they practiced the presence of God." As a result, their lives were not characterized by the anomie that so many people feel today.[11]

Evola, Bannon acknowledged, was "very authoritarian," noting, "he thought that democracy was a problem." But there is merit in his argument for traditionalism. "These traditions that have come down from the West from time immemorial about family, about belief, about culture," are critical to Evola, who "says of modernism, 'We have to reject this. Because this is going to take us to a place that de-humanizes us,'" Bannon said. Evola abhorred the dehumanizing role of technology, a caution that has as much relevance today as ever. "Modern transportation, modern media— I mean, you see it today. People feel less human, right? Because you're sucked up on the Internet," constantly clicking on the next thing and getting addicted to the little rush of gratification as a new website appears while divorcing yourself from the richness of the real world and eternal values. "All he was doing was trying to be a prophet that technology is shattering traditional civilizations.

And the traditional culture, traditionalist school, is what gives you that connection to the transcendent," Bannon said.

Guénon's *Man and His Becoming According to the Vedanta* is "a very powerful book for me," Bannon said. People get stuck on the "wheel of life," the daily churn and tyranny of routines that detach them from substantive, transcendent ideas and values. Though Bannon leads an Internet-based journalistic operation at Breitbart, he recognizes what a terrible influence the Internet can be. Guénon argues, Bannon says, that one must be able to come off the wheel of constant motion and reflect on where you are going. "Man is always becoming, right?" Bannon says. "You never reach the stasis, your whole life. And that became evident to me after I stopped drinking. That you have this time, and you have this work on yourself, you can always become better. You can always become more centered, you can always become more aware."

Evola and Guénon ultimately connect, for Bannon, to Gerard Groote, *The Imitation of Christ*, and *The Spiritual Exercises of St. Ignatius of Loyola*, and the notion of stopping to perform a daily "examen" and perceive what you are doing and where your life is going. "I'm not saying I've accomplished a lot in my life, but what I have accomplished is because of that set of practical tools that I was able to find," Bannon said. "People go, 'How did all this stuff come together?' Because I gave it conscious thought. I had the ability to really step back and really think it through."[12]

And for Bannon, thinking things through is not merely personal, it is about the history and future of the West, and most especially of his own country, the country that he served in the Navy, the country to which he has devoted all this historical study, and the country that he believes should put its own interests first and defend the culture that has made it so successful.

CHAPTER ELEVEN

Tea Party Warrior

In February 2009, CNBC correspondent Rick Santelli went into a tirade on the floor of the Chicago Mercantile Exchange, objecting to taxpayers' having to pick up the tab for "losers" who couldn't pay their mortgages. "We're thinking of having a Chicago Tea Party in July," he said. Santelli distilled the anger that was already growing among conservatives about what they perceived as a creeping government takeover of the country under Barack Obama. From sentiments such as these, the Tea Party movement was born.

For Bannon, the Tea Party was a populist vehicle for electing real conservatives who would oppose the otherwise relentless growth of government under Democrats and mainstream Republicans alike. The Tea Party embodied many of the most important aspects of Bannon's ideology. It was a movement of average Americans against the liberal establishment. It sought to roll back the state, cut taxes, and reassert our constitutional liberties. It unabashedly embraced the idea of "American exceptionalism"—that America was a uniquely blessed, exceptional country—and was suspicious of foreign military adventures and overseas nation-building.

Bannon believed that if America was going to retrieve its traditional culture, then the Tea Party *had* to succeed, because the Tea Party, in fact, *was* that culture, the dominant American culture of 1776 through the 1950s. "It's the voice of the working man and woman in this country," Bannon said during a February 2010 appearance on Sean Hannity's Fox News show. "It's the decent people who fight our wars, who run our civic organizations, who are the backbone of this country." It represented the people who had "1950s values," who wanted to "roll up their sleeves" and get to work. "Not looking for hand-outs," Hannity observed. "The exact opposite," Bannon agreed.[1] Bannon saw the Tea Party as a populist resurgence of such old-fashioned values as self-reliance, personal responsibility, fiscal prudence, freedom under the law, respect for American history and tradition, and patriotism opposed to the arrogance of internationalist, bureaucratic elites who wielded big government and big corporate power against them.

In the months leading up to the 2010 congressional elections, Bannon wrote and directed two films promoting the Tea Party. The first was *Fire from the Heartland*, which profiled the Tea Party movement and the women who were leading it; the second was *Battle for America*, in which Bannon pitted the Tea Party against what he viewed as Barack Obama's catastrophic presidency.

But these films were only part of his mission. Bannon became a determined, tireless advocate of the Tea Party and its principles. In late middle age, he was transformed into a full-time conservative activist. He became a founding member of the board of Breitbart

News and, after the death of Andrew Breitbart, its editorial director. He spoke at dinners and events where sometimes only a few dozen people would show up; he gave radio and print interviews, no matter how small the listenership or the readership, because he felt he had a mission to promote the Tea Party gospel to anyone and everyone he could and to return this country to its traditional values and principles; and in that mission, no audience was too small, no demand on his time was too great.

"I'm a conservative and I believe in the Tea Party movement," Bannon said during a 2010 interview promoting *Fire from the Heartland*. "I believe in our populist rebellion and I make films I think are of the highest artistic quality and I think that's been proven by people who've seen them and some of the comments they made....You know I'm 56 years old and I've changed my career now in my mid-fifties to be a [conservative activist] filmmaker full time." The Tea Party, Bannon said, "is the salvation of this country. It's the working men and women in this country."

Bannon urged those men and women to oppose not just Obama, but establishment Republicans who had no interest in stopping, and in fact were complicit in, the country's leftward drift. "November second is a very big day and we've got a very nasty, nasty fight in order to take control," Bannon said, referring to Election Day. "The morning of November third, we're going to have just as big a fight because the establishment, and particularly the Republican establishment, has no interest in making the fundamental changes in this country that we have to do in order to save our country." Bannon wanted voters to not only defeat liberals but to replace establishment Republicans with Tea Party Republicans who actually understood the nation's problems and were committed to doing something about them. "What we've got to do is, precinct by precinct, district by district, state representative by state representative, congressman by congressman—we have to take over the Republican Party."[2]

Fire from the Heartland was released September 22, 2010, to get Tea Party activists pumped up for the midterm elections, but, typically, the film approaches its subject in an off-beat way. *Fire from the Heartland* is actually a *feminist* movie, spoken entirely by women, focused on female empowerment, and highlighting the leading role of women in the Tea Party movement. That's right. Steve Bannon. Feminist. Not a single male voice is heard in the film, save that of Rick Santelli delivering a portion of his 2009 rant. Bannon believed that conservative women—or women who were conservative but hadn't yet realized it—had evangelical potential for the Tea Party movement.

"I think there's 70 percent or 80 percent of the country that actually support our values, and that's why I'm trying to make films like this," he said in September 2010. "Once people see films like that, a lot of women are sitting there, going, 'You know? I absolutely agree with the people I'm seeing onstage, they're just like me, and they believe in what I believe.' And I think that's why the left and the mainstream media are always trying to suppress this type of thing."[3]

Many of the women in the film would recoil from the term "feminist" because of its current political colorings. But the film is resolutely about women who were or are champions of the conservative movement, including the late Phyllis Schlafly, former congresswoman Michele Bachmann, and commentators like Ann Coulter, Michelle Malkin, S. E. Cupp, and Dana Loesch, among others. Unlike leftist feminists who see the state as their benefactor and radical social measures as "progressive," these women defend traditional values as pro-woman and reassert that America, and its constitutional liberties and limited government, is the best friend women ever had. "Motherhood is a political act," proclaims conservative journalist and gun rights advocate Dana Loesch in the film. Loesch said Tea Party women felt a responsibility to their children to join the fray. "They saw the future of their children at stake, and it would be completely disregarding their responsibility as a mother—their obligation to their children—to not pick a side and be active," she said.

"It isn't that men aren't seeing what's going on," Bachmann says in the film. "They are. But the difference is, women feel it. We feel it in our gut, our heart. And that sense is coming over us that something is terribly wrong." What was terribly wrong was that Barack Obama was leading an expansion of government power that was not just displacing the power and autonomy of individuals, families, communities, and churches, but imposing its "progressive" values over them. These women saw expansive government as an aggressor that needed to be stopped. "Women are the bearers of morality," says Coulter. "They're the transmitters of civilization. And liberalism is an attack on civilization, so you have the mama grizzlies getting their backs up. And a lot of the assault is moral, and it is cultural, and if you believe in God nothing scares you."

Christianity plays an important role in the film because Bannon and many of the women featured in *Fire from the Heartland* believe that liberalism is at war with Christianity and that Judeo-Christian morality is at the heart of America—and also the backbone of the Republican party. The film notes that the rights enumerated in the Constitution were assumed by the founders to be God-given, "unalienable rights" (in the words of the Declaration of Independence). The Constitution is meant to protect those rights. Liberalism, on the other hand, believes that rights come from the government, which can thus take them away if they conflict with the progressive agenda.

Liberals, for instance, want to marginalize the free exercise of religion guaranteed by the First Amendment. "They want to treat Christians like smokers. You can do it in your own home, but not out in any public place," Schlafly says in the film.

America "is manifestly an exceptional country," says Coulter. "And by the way, part of the reason for that, it was created and founded by Christians."

Bannon acknowledged that one intent of his film was to provoke the leftist women's movement. "The left...you know, their heads are imploding, because it's exactly against the narrative that they lay out about the feminist movement, and about the patriarchy, and how it suppresses women. Their worst nightmare has now come to fruition. It's that you've got a bunch of strong-willed, independent women at the vanguard of a populist, conservative rebellion against the political class and against the financial class."[4]

For Bannon, the leftist "women's liberation movement" was a foundation of the welfare state itself, providing a justification for statist policies—including subsidized abortion and birth control and single-motherhood—that either directly or indirectly assaulted the family that the "mama grizzlies" of his film were standing tall to protect.

"I think it goes against...the narrative of how they've built this entitlement state," he said in 2010. "And one of the central narratives of that is that there is a—which Phyllis Schlafly goes into in the film—that there's an oppressive patriarchy that suppresses women. They can't back away from that. I mean, that is the entire welfare state, the entire entitlement state is built around that. You know, the non-necessity of the family unit, the nuclear family, and marriage between a man and a woman. And really, a man being an actively engaged part of family life. And that cuts across everything they stand for. And so now, to see that you have this populist rebellion called the Tea Party, that fundamentally rejects many of the underpinnings of the modern socialist welfare state, and to have that led by articulate, tough…you know, 'not-gonna-back-down' women, is their absolute worst nightmare. And that's what they're confronted with. And heretofore…what they're trying to do is to stigmatize these women as crazy."[5]

Bannon was firing away at the solipsistic propositions with which liberal feminists had long fortified themselves. They believed they had a monopoly on what was right for women, and Bannon wanted to prove them wrong. And he was gleefully using strong, decidedly non-male-dependent women to do it. And to the extent he could score direct hits on the liberal women's movement, he could knock out one of the pillars of the broader evil he was seeking to upend, the welfare state that was stealing the culture upon which America had been founded.

While *Fire from the Heartland* promoted the Tea Party, his other September 2010 film *Battle for America* served as the bad-cop sibling to its sister film, dropping the hammer on Barack Obama and the Democrats in Congress. Urging viewers to get out and vote, it asserts that the future of the country is at stake and that the Democrats and Obama are contemptuous of the Constitution and traditional American culture.

"The stakes in this election are making sure that rebels against the statist and redistributionist trends are rewarded," says Arthur Brooks, president of the American Enterprise Institute, a right-leaning think tank. "It's a chance for us to remember that free enterprise is at the center of our culture."

The film had something of an all-star populist and traditional conservative cast, including Ann Coulter (again), Dick Morris, Fred Barnes, Newt Gingrich, Lou Dobbs, and Tom Coburn, and once more featured Bannon's eclectic approach to filmmaking, incorporating stock Hollywood footage of decadent, ancient Rome as a parallel to the statist ambitions and political decadence of Washington.

There's no way to know what role, if any, Bannon's films played in the electoral result, but the Republicans delivered what Obama acknowledged was a "shellacking," picking up sixty-three seats in the House of Representatives, while edging closer to a majority in the Senate with a gain of six seats.

Bannon enjoyed the Republican victory, but he had much more than congressional elections in mind.

CHAPTER TWELVE

The Palin Patriot

Bannon next turned his attention to creating an opening for the standard bearer of the Tea Party, Sarah Palin, to take power. Bannon first understood Palin's populist appeal when his sister called him during the 2008 campaign and said excitedly that she had just been to a Palin rally in Virginia where about twenty-five thousand people had arrived to see her. "I go, '25,000 people never show up in Virginia for anything.' She said, 'It's amazing. All the neighbors showed up.'"[1] In late 2010, Palin's people, after seeing *Fire from the Heartland*, approached Bannon about making a short video about her time as governor. He decided he had something grander in mind.

Bannon believed Palin was far smarter than people gave her credit for and that she had a particular genius for the things he knew needed to be done to transform Washington and change the direction of the country. And so he did what he knew best. He made a documentary about her. One problem was that she had lost the race for the vice presidency on the John McCain ticket and quit as governor of Alaska under siege from her antagonists. But she had taken a leadership role in the Tea Party and was as responsible as anyone for the massive Republican congressional victories in 2010. He called the film *The Undefeated.*

"I spent a year and a half observing her in the Tea Party Movement," he said. "We made this film in about nine months. So over two years really watching Governor Palin or seeing her in the whole movement of the Tea Party."[2] In Palin, Bannon had the American Dream story he loved above all others, a person from working class roots who rose and challenged those born to privilege and those exercising it. Palin was "Walmart nation," Bannon would say, and he meant it as a high compliment. What's more, Palin was someone who could galvanize people to action against established interests by both inspiring them and explaining in terms they could understand complex policies they had to embrace to wage the fight. Judging from how she governed Alaska, Bannon believed that Palin, unlike most Republicans, had the courage and conservative convictions to fight the Washington establishment, both Republicans and Democrats. She was genuine, without artifice, and would appeal to the middle-class voters Bannon believed were key to electing a Republican to the White House.

"The reason I was attracted to do the film about her, she identified this issue of a commercial, financial, and political class that have kind of melded together in what we call the permanent political class. It's a new aristocracy that perpetuates itself, that thinks about its own influence, its own power." Bannon later told a gathering of Palin's Grizzly Coalition at the CPAC Convention in 2012.

He timed the release of the film for July 15, 2011, to build support for Palin before the Republican primaries. Bannon said he wanted his film to dispel the mainstream media narrative that governor Palin was a "bimbo." A case in point for Bannon was how Palin had successfully explained her energy policies to the people of Alaska, plans that she argued would put the interests of Alaskans ahead of the interests of the oil companies. "It was very complex, very complicated, and she did it, and with overwhelming support. At the end of the day, these bills were passed by 48 to one margins," he said.[3]

That she could achieve this, Bannon asserted, was evidence that she could explain to American voters how the debt and deficit spending hurt the economy, raised unemployment, and were a giant danger to America's future. "What governor Palin did," in Alaska, was "she went around these little town halls with charts, and she explained to people the complexity of her tax policy," he said. "She explained to people this complicated way of how you bid to build this gas pipeline. And she did it in a very plainspoken manner. And by the way, once the citizenry understood what she wanted to do, they had her back."

This, to Bannon, was the test of an effective conservative politician—the ability to explain problems and rally the people to the appropriate solutions. It was just the kind of thing Ronald Reagan did—and Bannon's film, *The Undefeated*, frequently compares Palin to Reagan.

To make this argument was to fly against the leftist narrative, accepted as well by many on the establishment Right, that had been built against Palin. "The reason I made this film is that the meme [the Democrats and the mainstream media] had up there was this Caribou Barbie, who is a bimbo, and a right-wing ideologue," Bannon said. "Governor Sarah Palin is as smart as anybody that I went to Harvard Business School with, and she's as smart as anybody I worked at Goldman Sachs with. This is a very smart, tough, focused woman."[4]

The film, which is an unrelenting, heavy-handed, but fairly effective piece of pro-Palin propaganda, starts with her early career as mayor of Wasilla, Alaska, and moves on to her role as a state official and then governor fearlessly fighting entrenched, corrupt special interests. "No political establishment had propelled me to where I was," Palin says in the film. "In fact, I had reached the governor's office in direct opposition to the political establishment." The movie then covers her role in McCain's presidential campaign, including footage from her highly praised vice presidential acceptance speech at the 2008 Republican convention.

"Well, I'm not a member of the permanent political establishment," she said during her remarks. "And I've learned quickly these last few days that if you're not a member in good standing of the Washington elite, then some in the media consider a candidate unqualified for that reason alone. But here's a little news flash for those reporters and commentators: I'm not going to Washington to seek their good opinion. I'm going to Washington to serve the people of this great country."

The film glowingly describes her leadership of the Tea Party and makes the case that the reason she attracted so much media and leftist vitriol is that, unlike establishment Republicans, she was a real threat to the liberal Washington establishment-corporate media oligarchy. "America now has alternative, and Sarah Palin has offered that alternative, and [those in the liberal establishment] need to destroy her," says Andrew Breitbart in the film.

In promoting the documentary, Bannon acted almost as if he was Palin's 2012 presidential campaign manager. Bannon made the point that one of Palin's strengths as a politician was that she didn't get distracted from the big picture. "This woman did not go after school uniform problems" in Alaska, he said. "She cut the Gordian knot of problems that had not been solved in Alaska for

30 years," he continued. "She focuses on big problems that are [seemingly] intractable problems and comes up with solutions that many people can buy into."

Bannon warned that the Republican Party needed to be the representative of the Tea Party, because if it wasn't, it was doomed. "If the Republican party doesn't get tough enough and stand on the Tea Party conservative values, it will cease to exist as a party because the Tea Party will break off," he said. "It's the moral equivalent of the Whigs before the Civil War," Bannon said of the GOP establishment. "That is a party that has now gotten away from its roots and needs to have those rejuvenated. We need this primary to do that. I think it is incredibly important to have a primary like the [one in] 1976: President Reagan versus the establishment. We need to have a fight in the Republican Party for the soul of the conservative movement....We need to have this fight now."[5]

But in October 2011, a problem developed. Palin announced that she wasn't going to run for president after all. She had teased the country for months but ended up taking a pass. Bannon's candidate apparently had less stomach for political battle than he did. So he carried on without her.

Bannon wrote and directed three more documentaries in 2012, two of them focused on influencing that year's presidential election. The first, titled *The Hope and the Change*, premiered at the Republican National Convention. It featured commentary from forty Democrats and Independents who had voted for Obama in 2008 but now had severe cases of buyer's remorse. The film charts their move from excited participants in electing the first black president in American history to disenchantment as Obama's promises of hope and change seem to boil down to looking after the interests of the progressive elite.

The Hope and the Change was a well-crafted and effective documentary, but his second film of the year was superb. It was *Occupy Unmasked*, a dramatic exposé of the "Occupy Wall Street" movement. The film is a seventy-minute horror show that revives some of the themes of *Generation Zero* and links the sordid leftist violence of Occupy Wall Street to "community organizer" Barack Obama. The images are graphic, and they never stop. "There's raping and there's pillaging and there's pooping and the mainstream media ignores it," says Andrew Breitbart of the Occupy protests. Breitbart, the central speaker in the film, died within months of taping his part.

The film suggests the violence was directed by leftist radicals whelped during the 1960s, some of whom by 2011 were simply anti-American nihilists. "You pretend to be interested in issues," says David Horowitz, a former 1960s leftist who is now a conservative author. "You're a peace activist, you're a civil rights activist, you're upset about the financial crisis of 2008—nonsense. Your goal has always been the same, which is to destroy the society that you're alienated from...you basically hate America." It is the same thing some conservatives are saying of the "Antifa" movement in 2017.

After scenes of violence, chaos, foul language, rats, piles of garbage, burning buildings, angry faces, and smashed windows, former New York City Mayor Rudolph Giuliani delivers the punch line: "I believe that Barack Obama owns the Occupy Wall Street movement. It would not have happened but for his class warfare." We are reminded that Obama "worked as a community organizer," that he was an acolyte of Saul Alinsky, the godfather of modern radical leftist activism, and that he continued, as president, to speak the language of the radical Left.

The message is unmistakable: You cannot possibly reelect this man as president. But, a few weeks after the release of *Occupy Unmasked*, that's what America did.

So Bannon suffered two defeats in the 2012 election cycle—the withdrawal of his favored candidate, whom he had promoted to the best of his ability, and the reelection of Barack Obama—though actually he had predicted this. In a July 5, 2011, interview, Bannon forecast catastrophe should Republicans nominate someone like Mitt Romney, who was of course, exactly the candidate they chose. "If we want to get eviscerated, if we want to go back to 2008, let's run an establishment Republican like Mitt Romney, because we will get crushed," he said, months before Romney had even won a primary and while Palin was still a prospect. "We will lose the House, we'll lose more seats in the Senate. Nobody will show up in November, and not only will we get beat at the presidential level, we'll lose everything. We have to turn out the Tea Party. And the only way you're going to turn out the Tea Party is with a with a real Tea Party candidate. And so that's why I think that, honestly, I don't see anybody in the field that brings the energy, intelligence, or the dynamism of Governor Palin."[6]

The sky didn't fall quite as hard as Bannon had predicted. Democrats gained eight seats in the House and two seats in the Senate. But Barack Obama was comfortably reelected, and part of the reason was that, as Bannon had foreseen, too many conservatives stayed home.

Bannon wasn't done, though. What James Delingpole called "the eye of Sauron" was on the lookout for another Palin-like candidate who could revive the conservative movement and lead it to victory. "The beginning, really, of the Trump movement, was in Palin," Bannon told me.[7] Soon he would be in a position to help shape that movement—and the electoral results would be very different.

CHAPTER THIRTEEN

Bannon at Breitbart

After the Republicans, as Bannon had predicted, went down to defeat in 2012 running an establishment candidate, Bannon began looking ahead to 2016. This time, his tools for influencing the election would be more powerful than ever—even before he became executive chairman of the Republican nominee's campaign.

In March 2012, Bannon set up the Government Accountability Institute, the purpose of which is "to investigate and expose crony capitalism, misuse of taxpayer monies, and other governmental corruption or malfeasance." Bannon initially served as chairman and executive director, while his longtime collaborator, journalist Peter Schweizer, became GAI's president. With funding from Robert and Rebekah Mercer and other conservative philanthropists, Bannon wanted GAI to do the sort of "deep dive," data-driven, impeccably sourced investigative reporting that he felt was not being done—and to do it in ways that would compel the mainstream liberal media to pay attention. There were at least two ways to combat media bias. One was with alternative sources of information directed at conservatives, which is what the website Breitbart.com did. The other was to tempt liberal mainstream journalists with something they cherished almost as much as their bias—and that was well-sourced scoops. "What Peter and I noticed is that it's facts, not rumors, that resonate with the best investigative reporters," Bannon said, and he and Schweizer aimed to get those facts unearthed and distributed to reporters.[1]

GAI, then, wasn't just a partisan operation. It was a Bannon operation, devoted to exposing and taking down the corrupt Washington political establishment, or, as Bannon described it, "this permanent political class that has kind of crept up on the United States, both Republican and Democrat, that's really not accountable or answerable to anybody."

GAI's first three big investigations led to three bestselling books by Schweizer. The first, *Throw Them All Out*, was an exposé of rampant congressional corruption, including routinely practiced insider trading of the kind that is illegal on Wall Street. The second, *Extortion*, was explained in its subtitle, *How Politicians Extract Your Money, Buy Votes, and Line Their Own Pockets*. Both books went after Republicans and Democrats. The third book, and the most explosive, was focused on the Clintons, though as Bannon was quick to point out when the movie adaptation came out in the spring of 2016, "I think it's very important to go back and see the genesis of this, that we're not singling out Clintons per se in pursuing this, it's really an evolution of how this whole graft and corruption has developed over time." But that was just a little disingenuous. The book version of *Clinton Cash* conveniently landed in May 2015, just as Hillary Clinton was gearing up to run in the Democratic primaries for the nomination. And Bannon's documentary treatment of the book was released a year later, providing a second bite at the wormy apple of Clinton corruption just as she was preparing to face Donald Trump in the general election.

Clinton Cash was not only a bestseller in hardcover and reissued in paperback during the 2016 presidential campaign, but appeared in a bestselling graphic novel version as well before being made into a documentary feature by Bannon. The movie, and the book it was based on, did not play to emotion, but was relentlessly based on hard facts, and its intended audience was not just conservatives but Democrats who had every reason to suspect the corruption of candidate Clinton.

Bannon said of his movie, "I want as many progressives to see this as possible, because I think you have to understand how the Clintons, who proclaim that they support all your values, essentially have sold you out for money."[2] Progressives, Bannon knew, weren't going to vote for a Republican, but they had other options—either third party or simply sitting the election out—if they could be shown that Hillary Clinton was unworthy of their vote.

The movie *Clinton Cash* is such a dizzying catalog of Clinton corruption and alleged influence peddling that it begs the question of why the Democratic Party nominated Hillary Clinton as its party's presidential candidate. The film attempts, among other things, to connect big donations to the Clinton Foundation, and earnings from Bill Clinton's speeches, to the policies of Hillary Clinton's State Department, in what was, essentially, according to the film, a pay-to-play scam of enormous proportions and consequences. One of these alleged pay-to-play scams involved the Clinton State Department approving the sale of 20 percent of America's uranium deposits to Russia. But while Schweizer and GAI uncover a massive trail of evidence and help viewers connect the dots, the one thing missing is the smoking gun, the document that states definitively, in black and white, that Hillary Clinton was selling American foreign policy to the highest bidder. The evidence is weighty, but circumstantial, that donations to the Clinton foundation and six-figure speaking engagements for Bill Clinton influenced policy and State Department contracts under Hillary Clinton. GAI's research did get a mainstream hearing (part of it was done in conjunction with the *New York Times*), but it is, of course, hard to calculate what its electoral impact might have been or whether its allegations should have led to the appointment of a special counsel to investigate Hillary Clinton's conduct as secretary of state.

The other tool in Bannon's new toolbox with which he intended to wrench the presidency away from the Democrats was, of course, Breitbart.

*

Bannon had met Andrew Breitbart at the 2004 Liberty Film Festival. Bannon's film *In the Face of Evil: Reagan's War in Word and Deed* was shown there, and a young, excitable conservative named Andrew Breitbart was among those taking part in the panel discussions.[3]

After *In the Face of Evil* was screened, "the people went crazy," Bannon said. "Andrew Breitbart comes out of the crowd. He squeezes me like a grape. He literally comes out, he's a man's man, he grabs me, and like squeezes me like my head's going to blow. And he goes, 'You get it, culture's upriver from things. You're Leni Riefenstahl.' He's just going on and on. I'm like, who the fuck is this guy? He's a madman. I love him. He's a physical—he's a force of nature."[4] Bannon and Breitbart would eventually form an alliance based on shared conservative principles and an understanding of the media tactics needed to achieve victory in the culture war and in politics. They also harbored a similar energy, passion for the cause, and desire to make mischief. "I like to call someone a raving cunt every now and then, when it's appropriate, for effect," Breitbart once said, but the phrase could equally have been Bannon's.[5] Bannon helped Breitbart arrange funding for his website, including millions from wealthy conservative donors like Robert and Rebekah Mercer.

Breitbart died on March 1, 2012, at the age of 43. Bannon said of his fallen friend and ally: "In the vernacular of entrepreneurs, Andrew Breitbart simply 'got shit done.' Tons. Every day. All day. And had a helluva time doing it. And here is what made it more special: he didn't get 'shit done' for the powerful or the connected. It was, by and large, for those 'out of the loop' and marginalized."[6]

After Breitbart died, Bannon took over his website and began expanding it into its own force of nature, one that would lead the populist wing of the conservative movement. That, Bannon said, was what the website was for: to give the Tea Party its platform. Establishment conservatives and Republicans were as much the target as Democrats. Bannon was blunt: "We're never gonna beat the Democrats until we beat the real enemy, which is the establishment Republicans, because they stand for nothing. All they stand for is money and power, right? And we can take that on and defeat it."[7]

Bannon believed the mainstream media was a sham, that its claim to objectivity was belied every day by its blatant liberal bias. He described it to me as "a progressive, secular, humanist point of view, globalist in its nature" and that he intended Breitbart to be news source that was equally expressive of a worldview, a contrary worldview that was focused on defending the United States and Western civilization.

He started to build a journalistic team interested in crusading, sensationalist journalism. "I'm not looking for people who want to win Pulitzers," he said. "I'm looking for people who want to be Pulitzer," referring to Joseph Pulitzer, the hugely influential, muckraking nineteenth-century journalist and publisher.[8]

Bannon wanted to spur outrage. "You gotta play on the anger," he said. "The passion and the anger. No change has ever come to the world that anger wasn't built first. The American revolution— people were pissed. You gotta get them to get on the boat and throw the tea over the side."

Bannon wanted to rouse the blue-collar men and women who were good people with traditional values; patriotic, hard-working Americans who were tired of getting rolled over; men and women who were basically conservatives but left untapped by the establishment Republicans. "What you gotta do is bind those guys together and get them mad." To that end, Breitbart didn't focus too much on opinion pieces, it ran news stories, big stories often ignored by the mainstream media, that would get these blue-collar conservatives riled up. The goal was to "show" not to "tell," Bannon said. "Show them how it is. And by the way, they'll get so mad, and they'll keep coming back."[9]

Even establishment Republicans had adopted so many politically correct positions, and put so many politically correct restrictions on their own speech, that when Breitbart came out with articles like those on crimes committed by illegal immigrants in the United States or by Muslim immigrants in Europe, or criticized Black Lives Matter, it shocked a lot of people, no matter how true the stories were. America's media had reached a consensus that certain things, even certain truths, just weren't said. That gave Breitbart an opening to reach the millions of Americans who believed they weren't being told the truth. Breitbart also wasn't afraid to push the envelope of acceptable satire and bluntness with pieces like "Science Proves It: Fat-Shaming Works" or "Birth Control Makes Women Unattractive and Crazy" or by providing a platform for the flamboyantly homosexual, British, ethnically Jewish and self-proclaimed Catholic, conservative provocateur Milo Yiannopoulos (who penned those two pieces). More problematic for Bannon has been the website's association with the "alt-right," an amorphous and ill-defined group that some see as a band of modern, young, tech-savvy Brownshirts in designer glasses. Bannon told a journalist at the July 2016 Republican National Convention that Breitbart was "the platform for the alt-right."[10] Bannon told me that he hadn't seen the alt-right as racist. "The alt right, when it began, with Milo, at least I saw it, was just young, kind of almost libertarians, that were radical, you know, almost like patriots. These guys were the guys that kind of came from the chat boards, etc. And I said, they're going to be an amazing innovative force."

He added, "Building a successful media company online, a news organization, it is...a sedimentary rock. You have to build layers, and you have to have the social conservatives, and you have to have the libertarians, you have to have the limited government conservatives. You have to have the national defense hawks, you have to have the cultural warriors." And he believed the alt-right was just another conservative layer—and a vital one given its youth and spirit.[11]

Nevertheless, it was unmistakable that the alt-right contained some bad elements. Milo Yiannopoulos, a gay conservative activist who at the time was a writer for Breitbart, had published a piece in March 2016, four months before Bannon's "platform" comment, acknowledging a racist element to the alt-right. The worst of the group often made their appearance in the website's comments sections, which former editor Ben Shapiro called "a cesspool for white supremacist mememakers." For a long time, white supremacists and other evil minds were tolerated in the section, though the comments are now monitored. "Okay, the comment section at Breitbart got a little rough," Bannon admits. "It also got...I think it would be the number two- or three-sized comment section in the world," he boasted. "It is one of the reasons Breitbart exploded...the Darwinian environment of the comment section. And guess what? You're forewarned. You go to the comments section, you're an adult, it's Adult Swim. Okay? Don't go down there if you're a snowflake. Don't go down there if you're a precious flower. If you're a precious flower, you're probably not gonna be in the comment section." Bannon was dismissive of the racist element, saying it was insignificant and that, "All that crap gets burned out over time."

Bannon denies emphatically that he is racist or has any affinity for racists. Those who have known him best over the years, both liberal and conservative, back him up. "Friends, family and even now-critical former colleagues said the image of Bannon as a bigot is wrong," reported *The Washington Post*. "Bannon's longtime personal assistant is an African American woman, and he has extended family members who are Jewish," the *Post* noted. One might also look at Breitbart itself, which was founded by two Jews—Andrew Breitbart and CEO Larry Solov; has an orthodox Jew as one of its senior editors, Joel Pollak; and is ardently pro-Israel and has remained so under Bannon's leadership. Bannon's former screenwriting partner, Julia Jones has repeatedly told reporters that in more than a decade of working with him she had not detected any racism. "He is not a racist," said Jones, a self-described "Bernie Sanders" liberal.[12] "In the 14 years I've known him, I've never heard him utter a racist or anti-Semitic comment," said Peter Schweizer, another longtime collaborator. "As a woman, minority, an immigrant, and as a onetime supporter of Hillary Clinton, I believe I can be objective in my assessment of Steve Bannon," said Thai Lee, a Harvard Business School classmate. "The Steve I knew in the 1980s was a very smart, studious, and polite young man. I have never heard Steve speak ill of women, minorities, or others," she said.[13] And one of Bannon's former business partners in Hollywood, Jeff Kwatinetz, defended Bannon—at some risk to his career among the liberal movie business set. "If it hurts my career to tell the truth about someone, then I guess it's going to have to hurt my career, because he is a good person," Kwatinetz said in May 2017. "As a liberal, I don't judge people on their politics, I judge them on their character, and from what I knew then and what I know now, Steve has great character. He's not a racist or anti-Semitic. Things like that are absurd," he said. "He's a great person who wants the world to be a better place....Those beliefs aren't based on racism, they're based on what he honestly believes is best for the world."[14]

In his 2004 Reagan documentary, *In the Face of Evil*, produced long before he was publicly accused of being anti-Semitic, Bannon paid generous tribute to the Jewish film studio bosses who were the early pioneers of the art form he cherished, the cinema. In the documentary, the narrator describes the Hollywood system that gave Reagan his start. "This system did not happen by chance, but was the product of the grit, tenacity, and vision of a handful of Jewish entrepreneurs who had fled the destructive path of the Beast in early 20th century Russia and Eastern Europe. These visionaries differed in taste and style, yet shared two common elements: ruthlessness [which Bannon admires, of course, in a business sense] and uncompromising patriotism." "We are anything but racist," his sister Mary Beth told me. "It's just devastating," she said, to hear people make that accusation about her brother.[15]

Accusations of anti-Semitism stem from two things. Bannon's former wife, Mary Louise Piccard, claimed that he objected to their twins attending a school because there were too many Jews there. The girls went, however, and Bannon paid their tuition. The other so-called evidence was a Breitbart article provocatively titled "Bill Kristol, Republican Spoiler, Renegade Jew," but the whole point of the article, written by David Horowitz, himself a Jew, was that Kristol's opposition to Donald Trump, insofar as it benefited Hillary and the Democrats, was not only bad for the Republican Party but bad for Israel. "To weaken the only party that stands between the Jews and their annihilation [at the hands of Islamist terrorists], and between America and the forces intent on destroying her, is a political miscalculation so great and a betrayal so profound as to not be easily forgiven," Horowitz wrote. That was hardly an anti-Semitic sentiment.

Bannon sought to steel himself and his team against the opprobrium they would inevitably incur as a result of the populist-nationalist content they were creating. So he made Breitbart's unofficial motto, "Honey Badger don't give a shit," a reference to one of nature's fiercest, meanest creatures.

★

Bannon and the website weathered many controversies, but one that caused serious fallout happened on March 8, 2016, when Breitbart reporter Michelle Fields was grabbed by Trump campaign manager Corey Lewandowski. After a news conference in Jupiter, Florida, Fields chased after Trump to ask him a question, and someone grabbed her by the arm and pulled her away. The next day, Breitbart CEO Larry Solov published a statement: "It's obviously unacceptable that someone crossed a line and made physical contact with our reporter," it read. "What Michelle has told us directly is that someone 'grabbed her arm' and while she did not see who it was, Ben Terris of *The Washington Post* told her that it was Corey Lewandowski. If that's the case, Corey owes Michelle an immediate apology." On March 10, Fields wrote a brief account of the incident for Breitbart, saying that she was trying to ask Trump a question after he had been speaking with other reporters. "Trump acknowledged the question, but before he could answer I was jolted backwards," she wrote. "Someone had grabbed me tightly by the arm and yanked me down. I almost fell to the ground, but was able to maintain my balance. Nonetheless, I was shaken." While she may well have felt unsteady and nearly fallen after being jerked backward, the video does not show her starting to fall or being pulled toward the ground. That same day, she tweeted out a photo showing a bruise on her arm. The Trump campaign denied the incident, and Solov then issued a stronger statement: "We are disappointed in the campaign's response, in particular their effort to demean Michelle's previous reporting," he said. "Michelle Fields is an intrepid reporter who has covered tough and dangerous stories. We stand behind her reporting, her techniques, and call again on Corey Lewandowski to apologize."[16]

On March 11, Breitbart's Joel Pollak published a story saying that while Fields was grabbed by someone, the available evidence suggested it "was likely not" Lewandowski and noted that the campaign denied Lewandowski had done it. He said that Fields, who did not see who grabbed her, had "relied in good faith" on a witness. Updates during the afternoon acknowledged new evidence that showed Lewandowski reaching in her direction.[17] On March 13, both Fields and Breitbart editor-at-large Ben Shapiro resigned. "Today I informed the management at Breitbart News of my immediate resignation," Fields said in a statement. "I do not believe Breitbart News has adequately stood by me during the events of the past week and because of that I believe it is now best for us to part ways." Shapiro's resignation complained more broadly about Bannon using Breitbart to support Trump, while charging he had "abandoned and undercut his own reporter, Breitbart News' Michelle Fields, in order to protect Trump's bully campaign manager, Corey Lewandowski, who allegedly assaulted Michelle." By March 14, four more Breitbart employees had resigned.[18]

That evening, Fields and Shapiro appeared on Fox News. "I realized that my company didn't have my back," Fields said in explaining her decision to resign. "I can't stand with a company that won't stand for me. They knew the truth from the very beginning. My editor, as soon as it happened, had spoken to Corey. He told me that Corey has admitted to it and I was getting an apology so I stayed quiet. I wasn't going to make a big deal about it."[19] The *Daily Beast*, citing "sources," said that Lewandowski had admitted to the editor, Matthew Boyle, that he grabbed Fields.[20] Boyle denied the *Daily Beast* story.[21]

Bannon said his initial reaction to the event was, "Let's find out what's going on, and if Corey needs to apologize to her, somebody work it and apologize to her." He said Fields indicated to his staff that she was fine. But as the dispute continued, he said, "Let's just back off. Let's just step back from this thing and see how it develops." But then, when the video came out, he said, "It was like: are you kidding me? He barely touches her." Fields, in a recording of a conversation with Ben Terris of *The Washington Post* right after the incident, is heard saying, "That was insane. You should have felt how hard he grabbed me."

Bannon says Lewandowski acted because she was too close to Trump. He suggested Lewandowski overdid it, but that the response to what he did was too much. "So, she got too close to a candidate, [and] the guy's the chief of staff. Do I agree 100 percent with what Corey did? No," Bannon said. "Is Corey sometimes very headstrong? Yes. Absolutely. Does Corey not listen to people sometimes? Yes. All that stuff. Is Corey sometimes a rough piece of trade? Maybe. But that's the call of the people around him, right?"

It didn't, and still doesn't, seem to Bannon like what happened was such a big deal. "I thought the Michelle Fields thing, as history has shown, was totally overblown," he said. "And it also shows you the snowflake nature of the media. The meltdown the media had on this was all about getting Corey out as campaign manager because they wanted to destroy Trump. And I just thought it was a total joke. And by the way, it's part of the reason I have such complete contempt for the mainstream media. Because this has nothing to do with Michelle Fields, she was used."

What those who quit, for reasons that also went beyond Michelle Fields, hadn't understood was that Breitbart, under Bannon's leadership, was not merely about journalism—Bannon thought objective, disinterested journalism hardly existed anymore—it was about a mission, a cause. When Ben Shapiro wrote in his resignation statement that Breitbart had become "Trump's personal Pravda," the only proper response would be, "*Da, tovarish.*" And for Bannon, there wasn't a single thing wrong with it, because if his ideas were ever going to be realized and the Tea Party was ever going to seize power, the pro-Trump Republicans needed a media arm that would inform and rally their supporters and fight the propaganda of the Left and the mainstream media.

Just days after entering the White House, Bannon called the media "the opposition party." In July 2017, he told me they were even more the opposition than the Democrats. "They're totally confused, meandering around with no message," Bannon said of

Democrats. "The opposite, the media, is the opposition party. They stand diametrically opposed on Donald Trump's populist message, and against his nationalist messages. They are believers in open borders," he said, saying they are aligned with the "internationalists, globalists, the party of Davos, the centers of elites—New York, Washington, and Silicon Valley, Hollywood—that dominate our country."[22]

For the media, and Steve Bannon and Donald Trump, it would be total war.

CHAPTER FOURTEEN

Campaign Chief

Bannon first met Donald Trump in August 2010, as Trump was mulling a run for the presidency in 2012. Trump was talking with different Republican operatives and thinkers, and he wanted to understand what the Tea Party was all about. So David Bossie, who knew Trump, brought Bannon to Trump Tower in New York City. The conversation went on for hours. Bannon found that he and Trump, who in the end would not run in 2012, were kindred spirits ideologically. "Every one of these ideas were ideas he'd been talking about for 25 years," Bannon said. "On trade, on China, on the military—basically, he already had pretty well-formed his mind. Already, America First," Bannon said. "Now, on the social issues and immigration," Bannon added, Trump's ideas were not quite as well formed.

More than two decades before, as he tested the waters for a potential 1988 presidential run, Trump talked about having

America's allies pay their fair share for their national defense under America's nuclear umbrella. "We are a country that is losing $200 billion a year," he said during a speech in Portsmouth, New Hampshire. "We are supporting—we are literally supporting—Japan, which is the greatest money machine ever created, and we created it to a large extent. Let's not kid ourselves. We're supporting Saudi Arabia. We're supporting Kuwait. We're bringing in ships to Kuwait through the Gulf. We're losing our men. We're spending billions of dollars. So what's happening? They don't contribute one penny of this defense." Describing Iran as a "horrible, horrible country" and speaking more broadly about the Persian Gulf, Trump said, "Why couldn't we go in and take over some of their oil?" The United States "can't afford to be a whipping post."[1] During an appearance on *The Oprah Winfrey Show* in 1988, he sounded similar themes. "I think people are tired of seeing the United States ripped off," he said.[2]

When it came to politics, Trump and Bannon had followed similar trajectories—from holding some old-style Democratic ideas to becoming populist-nationalist Republicans. The two had personal similarities as well. Both were successful dealmakers in business. Both seem to thrive on rhetorical, business, or political combat. And both have been card-carrying members of the very establishment against which they rebelled—Bannon with his background at Goldman Sachs and in investment banking and Hollywood finance, and Trump as a real estate magnate. "I came at it from building companies throughout the world and then finally working in film and news media. He came at it from being a practical, global businessman in real estate, and a TV guy," Bannon said.

Once Trump started appearing on the campaign trail in 2015, Bannon found that the candidate had powerful rhetorical skills.

He understood that Trump, uniquely, could connect with the very people he knew a successful campaign would have to target: average, middle- and working-class voters. "He doesn't speak like a politician. He speaks like an average person. And it resonates," Bannon told me. "His connection is a visceral connection, because of his success, and they hold him in high esteem for his success, but he is one of them. He is a reflection of them, and he speaks to them in their own language."

Trump had something that Bannon knew was rare in politics and hardly detectable in Washington. He had authenticity. It was what had drawn Bannon to Sarah Palin, who lacked sophistication and had little of Bannon's own erudition, but who could inspire average people, assuring them that she wasn't the usual preening, self-serving politician. Bannon understood that you could not lead a populist revolt against the establishment if you didn't have a candidate who could connect to the actual populous. And now here was another outsider who resembled Palin in many ways, but who, unlike her, was willing to make a go of an arduous presidential campaign.

Despite his vast wealth, Donald Trump was a man of the people. He spoke to their concerns; he spoke their language; he talked off the cuff with disarming directness; and he was unafraid of the media or of saying politically incorrect things he believed to be true. He was colorful, larger than life in some ways, but also down to earth. He seemed without pretense. In a campaign where Hillary Clinton dodged a friendly media, Trump met regularly with a hostile press for much of the campaign. He was a happy warrior. He had the courage of his convictions. And he was genuine, speaking about issues that he felt really mattered to working people, ignoring all the poll-driven, focus-group-driven advice of the political class fearful of offending anyone.

Bannon is scathing about the "thinness" of the political rhetoric of most politicians, all of whom have carefully "test-marketed" specific words they allow themselves to use. Bannon says that voters see through that, and wanted a change; they wanted someone who will tell them the truth and not hide behind buzzwords and phrases. "The point is," he told me, that if you campaign like that, using campaign consultant language, rather than speaking honestly, "you don't have faith in the American people. Basically, the folks I was raised around, the blue-collar, lower-white-collar class are very smart," he said. "Working-class people are just as smart— at the end of the day—as the elites about what's really important in the world. All you have to do is talk about those issues." But modern political speech, he said, was designed "*not* to talk about the issues." It was about a series of evasions that were meant to keep voters pacified while the political class looked after its own interests.

Trump talked about issues that establishment politicians didn't: the erosion of American sovereignty, the swamping of American culture by illegal immigration, unfair trade practices that hurt working-class Americans, especially in manufacturing. Not one of these issues is popular in Washington.

Trump's willingness to depart from the standard political script was one reason the Washington elite, so acclimated to sterile test-marketed verbiage, was so aghast at Trump. "All these guys were like, 'Oh my god! This is so shocking!'" said Bannon. But these were the things that were on the minds of average citizens every day. "Trump literally is providential, in that he understood, because he's an expert in mass communications, in a much more sophisticated level than anybody I ever met, how to use a plain-spoken language to talk about central issues and connect with a working-class audience."

Bannon also thought this approach was how the Republican Party could in due course win minority voters and why he thought the plan for wooing Latinos in the "autopsy" report prepared by the Republican National Committee after the 2012 election was bunk. Bannon believed that rather than playing identity politics with Hispanics, which inevitably involved pandering on different issues, Republicans should campaign for Hispanic votes on the same issues that mattered to all working people, including making the case that enforcing the nation's immigration laws was in their interest. "The reorganization of the Republican party into a worker's party, that's what I focus on every day," Bannon told me. "And I keep telling people. Once we get 25 percent or 30 percent of the black working class, once we get 25 percent or 30 percent of the Hispanic working class, we're gonna govern for 100 years. I come from a black neighborhood. They're conservative people. More conservative than the radicals I see coming out of the Cato Institute. You give me the Cato Institute versus a black, working-class neighborhood...[and I'll take] the black working-class neighborhood," because it is workers, not libertarian theorists, who "are the backbone of the country."

How do Republicans win black voters, who vote against them nine to one? "You get them by showing that we're going to support the protection of American industries. We're going to help nurture and grow American industries." Bannon believes the key to building Republican strength among blacks and Hispanics is by building an economy that can sustain working class jobs, which is one motivation behind Trump's push to rebuild America's infrastructure.[3]

In fact, one of Bannon's tasks during the campaign was making the case to blacks and Hispanics that Trump's policies on trade and illegal immigration would directly benefit them, and provide more jobs. In the end—to the astonishment of the media, the Democrats, and establishment Republicans—Trump did slightly better with black and Hispanic voters than Mitt Romney did in 2012, laying the groundwork for a post-Trump Republican candidate less vilified by the media (and his own party), but following the same policies, to do even better than Trump.

The future of the Republican Party, Bannon told me, is in appealing to the average American—something that the Democrats, in their pursuit of identity politics, and with their ever greater radicalism, cannot do. "The greatest power we've had in the destruction of the Democratic Party is the creation of 'the resistance.' Particularly, it's the aspect of the multicultural, open borders, illegal immigration" Democratic Party, a party that has embraced "everything that's destroyed" its own ability to offer a nationalist platform. If the Democrats "can create democratic nationalism as a counter, we'll be in a fight for power for the next 50 years. If we take that off the table, we own them as a party. They will never be able to regroup. They will stay in their identity politics and continue to lose, and lose, and lose, and lose. And the more gasoline we throw on the resistance, the more they freeze up."

Bannon welcomed the fire he drew from Clinton during the campaign and the fire he continued to draw from the media and the Left once he was in the White House. "I knew we had Hillary and her campaign right at the beginning. I'd been announced," as new campaign chief, and "I think three days later she came out to make a big speech, and the speech was about the alt-right, Bannon, and Breitbart," he said. "I realized right then we had her. Because you're going right to identity politics [and] it's a cul-de-sac. What are they complaining about Hillary today? She never tackled the economic issues."

★

The first thing Bannon did after taking over the campaign on August 17, 2016, was to get "some order" into it. "I knew what I had to do. It was messaging, scheduling, and ground game," he told me. "And so on messaging, it was just, throw out everything else that they had." And get Stephen Miller—Trump's speech writer, with whom Bannon was already close and ideologically aligned—to craft speeches relentlessly hammering home a populist, nationalist message and imprint on voters that Hillary Clinton was the establishment and Trump was the agent of change. And don't pussyfoot around. "A hardcore nationalist message. A hardcore populist message," Bannon said. "She's the representative of an elitist, ineffective, corrupt status quo. He is an outsider agent of change, he's a businessman."

Oh, and, "It's the Economy Stupid." Bannon didn't use the old 1992 Bill Clinton internal campaign mantra, but he knew that Trump had to stick to economics. In fact, his speeches would from now on be filled with policy. "When I first started covering Trump at the start of his campaign, he was a candidate of gut instincts," said *Washington Post* reporter Robert Costa. "It wasn't until Bannon came on in August of 2016 that you really saw Trump, working with Sessions and Bannon, start to put policy to his gut instincts."[4]

Bannon found some people who could help. Washington communications veteran Sean Spicer was brought in "on loan" from his post as Republican National Committee communications director and strategist, while RNC chief of staff Katie Walsh was also given a central role. On the recommendation of Jared Kushner, Trump's son-in-law, he hired Bill Stepien, a former aide to New Jersey Governor Chris Christie, who would oversee voter turnout.

And he hired his old aide-de-camp, David Bossie, to be deputy campaign manager. "Those four kind of became the core team," Bannon said.

The campaign was down 16 points and, worse, according to Bannon, Trump was in the low 70s among Republicans, and he had to get that number up to 90 percent if he wanted to have any hope of winning. Too many were turned off by the controversial GOP standard-bearer. Bannon did several things to try to change this. They all centered on one principle: "Give people permission to vote for Trump." Many voters had their problems with him, but if they had enough reasons to vote for him, and enough reasons not to want Clinton, they'd pull the proverbial lever for him anyway.

First and foremost was to drill home the nationalist message Bannon believed would inspire middle-class Republicans, and to turn Trump's lack of political experience into an advantage, to present the outsider Trump as a man who could effect real change and contrast him with the corrupt insider Clinton who represented the establishment political class.

But Bannon also decided that the campaign had to be careful to highlight traditional Republican messages that would appeal to traditional conservatives, such as emphasizing the conservative judges that Trump would appoint. "Put enough Republican stuff in there about the courts, about all that stuff that they would say, 'Hey, Donald Trump's terrible, but he's not Hilary Clinton,'" Bannon said. Bannon believed there were plenty of issues in Trump's platform—from the courts to deregulation to tax reform to boosting the nation's military—that could be deployed to convince reluctant Republicans to vote for Trump.

But the campaign's greatest asset was Trump himself. The campaign gave him great stages on which to work his magic with crowds. "He's like William Jennings Bryan," Bannon said, comparing Trump to perhaps the most electrifying populist stump speaker in American history. Trump had a charisma that, in its own way, matched that of Jack Kennedy, Ronald Reagan, and Bill Clinton.

Charisma had been one of Trump's secret weapons over his rivals in the Republican primaries (Jeb Bush, Ted Cruz, John Kasich, Marco Rubio, and the rest proved to be a remarkably uncharismatic bunch) and Hillary couldn't get any of it to rub off from Bill.

"Trump has a visceral connection with people," Bannon said. "One of the reasons is physical charisma, his presence. The Greeks said it's a gift. A gift from the gods. If you're in a room with him, he takes over a room. God, it's unbelievable. I've never seen anybody like him. He has a physically dominating presence that is much bigger than his own size," which at a broad-shouldered six feet two can already be intimidating.

Trump's presence on the stage would be amplified by his gigantic presence on Twitter. Social media would multiply the message in his speeches and help him circumvent the baying critics in the media by letting him speak directly to his tens of millions of followers.[5]

Jared Kushner had another great idea that Bannon embraced: send Trump to Mexico. It would not only highlight the immigration issue, but it would make Trump seem presidential. And what could be more emphatic permission to support a candidate for president than making him seem presidential? Traveling south of the border on August 31, 2016, Trump played to two different audiences. Meeting with Mexican president Enrique Peña Nieto in Mexico City, he was subdued and dignified, not even getting into it with Peña Nieto when the Mexican leader informed Trump that Mexico would not pay for Trump's border wall, as Trump had been insisting during the campaign.

Howard Wolfson, who had run Clinton's communications shop during the 2008 Democratic primaries, tweeted: "If you believe Trump needed to pivot, moderate and look more Presidential, that event was a home run." But a few hours later in Phoenix, Trump let it rip, getting right back to playing to the base. "Anyone who has entered the United States illegally is subject to deportation," Trump declared. By the end of that day, polling showed that Trump was just four points down.

Trump was getting close to Clinton despite his own occasionally outrageous statements and the constant attacks from the media. In the 1980s, the press characterized Ronald Reagan as "the Teflon president" because all the criticism that was hurled at him just seemed to slip right off the genial commander-in-chief. Ironically, Trump's unvarnished nature provided similar protection. Democrats were forever frustrated that few of the arrows they slung his way ever stuck. Even he marveled at his ability to absorb attacks that would sink other candidates. "I could stand in the middle of 5th Avenue and shoot somebody and I wouldn't lose voters," he said during the primaries. Reagan's success shocked the press, liberals, and even the Republican establishment, but that was nothing compared to their utter discombobulation at the rise of Trump.

Worse, to them, was that his outrages only seemed to make him stronger. For voters sick of the status quo, Trump's mistakes and bad press only underlined that he was not part of the corrupt political establishment and not a typical politician—so it often became a positive. He made outrageous mistakes because he said what he thought and not something programmed. And given that he withstood such a battering from the media, the Democrats, and his own party—and triumphed over them all—he was certainly not "fragile," to use a term made popular by Nassim Nicholas

Taleb in one of Bannon's favorite books, *Antifragile*; Trump was one of those forces of nature that grow stronger from stress and negative stimuli, in Taleb's vocabularly not just robust, but "antifragile."

Hillary, by contrast, was brittle. She was the favorite, the one who was supposed to win, and her campaign was trading off her vast experience as a first lady, senator, and secretary of state. She presented herself as the sane and reliable candidate whose supporters didn't have to like her but were commanded to respect her. "From Baghdad and Kabul to Nice and Paris and Brussels, from San Bernardino to Orlando, we're dealing with determined enemies that must be defeated. So it's no wonder that people are anxious and looking for reassurance. Looking for steady leadership," she said in her Democratic National Convention acceptance speech on July 28, 2016.

"So just ask yourself: Do you really think Donald Trump has the temperament to be commander-in-chief? Donald Trump can't even handle the rough-and-tumble of a presidential campaign. He loses his cool at the slightest provocation—when he's gotten a tough question from a reporter, when he's challenged in a debate, when he sees a protestor at a rally. Imagine, if you dare imagine, imagine him in the Oval Office facing a real crisis. A man you can bait with a tweet is not a man we can trust with nuclear weapons," she said. "America's strength doesn't come from lashing out. It relies on smarts, judgment, cool resolve, and the precise and strategic application of power. That's the kind of commander-in-chief I pledge to be."[6]

As the campaign wore on, Hillary seemed to be astonished and appalled and frustrated that she could not put Trump away. She criticized him for not being thoughtful and talking about the issues, while she herself emphasized how Trump had allegedly been rude to a former beauty queen. She tried to dismiss him as an ignorant, racist, sexist bigot who represented "the deplorables." She did not come across as someone who was maintaining her cool, but as someone who was herself in fact fragile, who was suffering from the stress of campaigning, and who was condescendingly angry that she even had to contest the election against such an opponent.

Trump, however, at his rallies and then, finally, in his election night victory, appeared a tower of strength, whether one admired him or not. "They look like the incarnation of 'antifragile' people," Taleb said of the incoming members of Trump administration. "The definition of 'antifragile' is having more upside than downside," Taleb added. "For example, Obama had little upside because everyone thought he was brilliant and would solve the world's problems, so when he didn't it was disappointing. Trump has little downside because he's already been so heavily criticized. He's heavily vaccinated because of his checkered history. People have to understand: Trump did not run to be Archbishop of Canterbury."[7]

What's more, Hillary Clinton's strategy of holding herself up as a paragon of steadiness was risky for a woman who had been under federal investigation twice, who had been known for throwing lamps around the White House, and whose health seemed very uncertain, including collapsing as she fled a public event.

★

Trump's and Bannon's strategy was actually driven far more by ideas than Hillary Clinton's was, despite the snickering of the intelligentsia that Hillary was facing off against the Visgoths. They had a shared ideological vision of what really mattered to most Americans, which was backed by a crucial demographic insight. The Democrats played identity politics by pandering, in an ever more divisive way, to Americans on the basis of race and sex and sexual orientation, and even irreligion. In the process they had abandoned the sort of white, blue-collar workers who had once been the party's backbone. Democrats had gotten swept up with the idea of the "browning" America and seemed to assume that the white working class was one demographic group they could take for granted or ignore. That proved to be a fatal mistake. These were precisely the voters that Trump and Bannon energized with their populist-nationalist platform. Writing in June 2013 for the website RealClearPolitics, Sean Trende noted the often overlooked fact that the white population was, in fact, still growing. Much of the focus by the "smart" analysts, including those in the Republican establishment, was on the decline of whites as a share of the population. That was true. But in a fascinating analysis, Trende calculated that the number of white votes cast should have increased between 2008 and 2012 by about 1.6 million because of population growth. It didn't. Uninspired by Romney, white voters, who trend Republican, stayed home. In fact, there were more than six million fewer white voters in 2012 than should have been expected. But the key issue was, "these voters were largely downscale, northern, rural whites." These were the voters who helped propel Trump to his eventual victories in Pennsylvania, Michigan, Wisconsin, and Ohio.

Trende noted, prophetically, that if these white, blue-collar, rural voters turned out in 2016, "we're in the ballpark of being able to see a GOP path to victory." To win these voters, Trende wrote, the GOP would have to abandon "some of its more pro-corporate stances." Moreover, "This GOP would have to be more 'America first' on trade, immigration, and foreign policy; less pro–Wall Street and big business in its rhetoric; more Main Street/populist on economics." Trende noted, however, that "For now, the GOP seems to be taking a different route, trying to appeal to Hispanics through immigration reform and to upscale whites by relaxing its stance on some social issues. I think this is a tricky road to travel, and the GOP has rarely been successful at the national level with this approach." Trende acknowledged that this conventional approach might work. Nevertheless, he noted that while "it's certainly the route that most pundits and journalists are encouraging the GOP to travel," this "might tell us more about the socioeconomic standing and background of pundits and journalists than anything else."[8]

Bannon was well aware of Trende's analysis and was bullish. Trende "went back and did all this analysis...pulling data and literally gave us the map to 2016," Bannon said.[9] But Bannon had yet more data to back up his approach, and this came from August 2014 polling done by one of his closest associates on the campaign, Kellyanne Conway, which showed Trump's immigration stance, the centerpiece of his campaign, was a winner, no matter what elite opinion in Washington thought.

"Americans are more focused, and more opinionated on the issue of immigration than in recent years," she wrote in a memo describing the poll. "Likely voters were unequivocal in their support of immigration policies that protect the American worker." That was music to Bannon's ears. Conway continued: "Seventy-five percent want more enforcement of current immigration laws, including 63 percent of Hispanics and over 50 percent of Democrats," the memo stated. "There is strong consensus on many populist immigration policies," including: "Strengthen enforcement of current immigration laws; encourage returning or staying home by tightening access or eliminating public benefits to illegal immigrants—at least adults—and improve enforcement of employment laws; limit chain immigration for legal immigrants to immediate nuclear family; encourage/require businesses to hire American citizens and legal immigrants already here first." She said the analysis turned "on its head" the "cynical meme that legal and illegal immigrants do the jobs Americans won't do." For a candidate to come out and state this truth: that immigration law should give preference to American workers "would be a public relations coup. The idea that Americans should do—and should be preferred in trying to do—the jobs currently held by immigrants—enjoys broad public support."[10] Conway had the data to back up this statement, but she also had a gut political sense from her own rural and working-class roots in New Jersey. A nationalist-populist campaign that focused on putting Americans first and enforcing our immigration laws would energize these voters.[11]

Not many in the GOP establishment understood or believed in Trump's strategy, but Ross Douthat, a *New York Times* columnist and a moderate-conservative Never-Trumper, wasn't far off when he projected what he termed an unlikely but plausible path to victory for Trump. "Trump needs to turn out a lot of people (working-class whites, in particular) who rarely or almost never vote," Douthat wrote. "The American Electoral College is an unusual system, and Trump is an unusual candidate. He's likely to underperform among normal Republicans in many red states, where the white working class is already very Republican, by losing white suburban professionals who voted for John McCain and Mitt Romney. But he might overperform in Rust Belt states where the white working class is still a residually liberal swing vote, and where there are a lot of disaffected independents who sat out 2012.

"This unusual combination—underperforming but still probably winning Republican states, possibly over-performing in purple states—suggests a true black swan endgame: Not Trump 44, Clinton 43, but Clinton 45, Trump 43...except that Trump, with his

Rust Belt strength, loses a lot of reliable deep-red votes he doesn't need and turns out just enough nonvoters in a few key swing states to take the Electoral College 270-268."

Douthat added, however, "No, it's not likely. No, don't freak out."[12]

★

But Bannon knew it could be done, and he thought it was likely. He had seen how the Tea Party populist wave had swept Republicans into power in 2010. He knew how a similar populist wave had launched the Reagan Revolution. He knew how Phyllis Schlafly had led a populist movement to defeat the Equal Rights Amendment, showing that grassroots conservatives could, in her own words, spoken in Bannon's *Fire in the Heartland*, "win over enormous odds." Bannon, as campaign chief, repeatedly told Trump his chances of winning were "100 percent." After the 2005 *Access Hollywood* videotape emerged of Trump telling host Billy Bush that he grabbed women "by the pussy," even Trump himself wasn't so sure. "Come on, it can't be a hundred percent," Trump said to Bannon. "No, it's a hundred percent," Bannon replied, even as some on the campaign thought the candidate's chances had been wrecked. "Just stick to your message," Bannon told him. "Stick to this nationalist message, stick to the populist message, stick to the fact that she is the establishment, she is the status quo," Bannon said. "You're an agent of change. People are thirsting for change. We know that all we have to do is give them permission to vote for you. You give them permission to vote for you, you're gonna win."

Recalling the lessons of *The Fourth Turning*, Bannon also believed history was on Trump's side, that the time had come for a strong character to resist the demands of the politically correct and steer America back to the core values it had abandoned in the 1960s. "It's one of the reasons I got so involved and so admired Trump and the courage he had," Bannon said.[13] The change needed to be dramatic. Trump, Bannon had said, was a "blunt instrument" that could effect it.[14] He had the passion, the unconventionality, and the work ethic that were required. Would charter members of the establishment without a whiff of originality like Marco Rubio or Jeb Bush save the nation from its peril? Not a chance. They didn't even see the problem. Actually, for Bannon, people like Bush were part of the problem.

But Bannon believed that with Trump as president, it was possible that the nationalist, populist ideology Bannon had formulated over years of reading and thinking could be established—or more accurately, re-established—in the United States. During the Fourth Turning, when the country enters a crisis period—as it was well into by 2016 after the 2008 financial collapse—the establishment gets marginalized so that fresh blood can come in and solve the problem. "The most powerful thing for me of the Fourth Turning, was that, and which dovetailed with my study of history, is that when crises come, that the big kahunas and the guys that are like the know-it-alls and everything like that, and the go-to guys at the beginning of the crisis, all fall away to be nobodies," he said. "You never hear about them in history." Bannon cited the rise of Abraham Lincoln and Ulysses S. Grant to save the United States during the Civil War, and the accession to power during World War II of Winston Churchill, who in the 1930s had appeared to have landed on the scrap heap of history.

"All these other guys see different aspects of it," Bannon said of those who take power during a Fourth Turning. "It's both Trump and Bannon, and others in a crisis. You know, Trump was a reality TV guy. Think how the media mocked him. Dismissed him." Bannon suggests his own confidence in the need for disruptors allows him to brush off the constant attacks lodged at him by the establishment. "That's why I laugh at the *Morning Joe* thing," Bannon said of the MSNBC show, whose hosts Joe Scarborough and Mika Brzezinski often mock Bannon and Trump. "They are the conventional wisdom."

When Bannon showed Trump an article about the Fourth Turning in April 2017, the president wasn't so sure he liked it. "Man, that's very dark," Trump said. "You know, I'm very optimistic." Bannon tried to reassure him. "It's not supposed to be dark," he said. "It's just supposed to be a theory of how history rolls out. It clearly is optimistic because, at the end of the day, America finds a solution and goes to the next level."

"Let's connect 2009 to 2016," Bannon said. "What we had was that the little guy in the street revolted. This 2016 vote absolutely came from that moment. And the campaign was run like that! These elites had never been held accountable."[15]

Now they would be held accountable. As Trump completed his victory speech on November 9, 2016, with Bannon onstage a few yards to his left, the Rolling Stones' 1969 song "You Can't Always Get What You Want" began playing, as it often had during the campaign, somewhat incongruously. It was an anthem of the era whose values Bannon had spent most of the past decade working to banish from the culture. Now, having ascended from working-class Richmond, Virginia, to the summit of power, he would have his chance.

CHAPTER FIFTEEN

The President's Strategist

Bannon's office in the White House was relatively small, but in the West Wing, the traditional real estate maxim is truer than anywhere else: *It's location, location, location.* Bannon worked just two doors down from Trump, with only the office of the president's son-in-law, Jared Kushner, between his and the Oval Office.

Before General John Kelly became chief of staff, the Trump White House was a freewheeling place and Bannon could walk just a few paces down the hall and talk to the president of the United States almost anytime he wanted.

Bannon speaks almost reverentially of Trump; in the White House, to other aides, he routinely referred to him as "the boss"; and he noted to me how easy it was for Trump to strike awe in those around him: "I've never seen anybody like him," Bannon said.

But Bannon could also be direct with Trump, be frank with him, and even confront him when he thought it was necessary. It helped that they shared a similar vision of the world and even a similar sense of humor; and they think alike, routinely finishing each other's sentences.

"What [Trump] really wants to do is smoke cigars," a Republican close to the White House told *The New Yorker*. "But the family is telling him, 'Smoking cigars is really bad for you and the doctor told you not to do it.' He's, like, 'I know, I know.' So when he's around his family, he's, like, 'Look, I'm not smoking cigars!' And then he goes off with his golf buddy. And guess what they do? They fucking light up cigars, because that's actually who he is and what he thinks. And Bannon is like his golfing buddy that he goes and smokes cigars with. That's actually who he is."[1]

Bannon was very much an advisor; he was not the brains behind the president, as some alleged. Bannon told me that Trump "is very engaged. He knows the big ideas he's trying to get out." And he also likes to gather different points of view. As Bannon put it, Trump "comes to his conclusions by the Socratic method." The opinions he seeks are not just those of the Washington insiders. "What he does is a continual questioning of a wide range of people. He'll ask the experts, but he will get opinions from his friends, from various business colleagues, people he respects." He's also not bound by conventional thinking. "He'll ask off-the-wall questions about things," just to probe all the angles and find an original approach. "He doesn't just absorb information by...getting 200-page briefing papers." Bannon argues that contrary to what Trump's critics think, his manner of gathering information and coming to a conclusion is "very learned and very deep, and particularly learned in the understanding of human nature and of how the world works, which to me, is everything." And no, Bannon says, Trump doesn't take the advice of the last person he talks to, as has been suggested many times in the press, nor is he easily fooled. "If you try to limit the information he gets, if you try to sell him something, he's savvy enough to know—because he's a salesman—when he's being sold."[2]

During the Republican primaries Bannon never bought into the establishment conservative media's portrayal of Trump as a malleable opportunist. On the contrary, he regarded Trump as the one Republican presidential candidate with the intestinal fortitude and depth of belief to stick to his campaign program. He believes that view has been mostly confirmed, as Trump has governed by conservative policy principles, and has been consistently to the Right of a Republican Congress that itself looks ideologically suspect, lacking in belief, and initimidated by the Left. After Trump won the election, many in Washington figured that the establishment could get back to business as usual. Part of the incredible hostility to Trump is that he is sincere in wanting to "drain the swamp" of the Washington bureaucrats and spendthrifts and is unabashed at taking on the media and the Left, refusing to kowtow to their agenda.

"There's a phrase I'm going to use that will shock you, that you never thought anybody would put together: Donald Trump and moral courage. I have never seen someone I admire...more than Trump," Bannon told me in July 2017. "The pressure on Trump right after he won was amazing, intense, and from every different direction—from the business community, from his friends, from the tech community—to moderate, to change, to not do this, to not do that, to go be loved, to do a whole lot of other things...than what he committed to the American people, to the 'deplorables.'" Trump stuck to the commitments he ran on. "That is the story of this administration," Bannon said. "I've had a ringside seat."[3]

Bannon acknowledged that some items on the agenda were reconsidered once Trump had taken up residence at 1600 Pennsylvania Avenue, not because he lacked commitment but because some members of the administration had other ideas, to which he felt he should listen. "There are a number of people who really weren't with Trump, who kind of came into the administration—and they're good people, don't get me wrong—and they have very strong opinions," he said. But, for the most part, Trump was not backing down.

Bannon put the best face he could on Trump's initial decision to bring establishment Republicans like Reince Priebus and Sean Spicer, and even Democrats, into the White House. "He's very obviously attracted to success," Bannon said. "He's very attracted to having smart people around. Donald Trump does not look for sycophants." Bannon even offered some praise for a man viewed as one of his chief antagonists in the White House, National Economic Council Director Gary Cohn, who is a Democrat. "I like Gary a lot," Bannon said. "I mean, we absolutely are at the opposite ends of the spectrum, as far as our beliefs. But he's a fighter. Trump says he's a killer. He fights for his stuff."

Bannon acknowledged that he respected Trump's preference for getting many contrasting views on policy. "I believe that it's not bad to debate ideas," he said. "I'm a big believer in the Darwinian nature of the debates on ideas. That the best idea wins."

The strength of Bannon's position in the White House was that he was Trump's alter ego, often confirming his instincts, providing an intellectual and ideological framework for them, and someone Trump could talk with about the strategy and tactics of constructing actual policies.

Bannon has been compared to George W. Bush advisor Karl Rove and Barack Obama confidante Valerie Jarrett—and perhaps could be compared to Bill Clinton's shadowy consigliere Bruce Lindsey—as the person who "gets" the president and was his most trusted aide. But Bannon, with his famous whiteboard listing all of Trump's campaign promises, was actually more than that. Those advisors were essentially tacticians. Bannon is that, but also a strategist, a visionary, a political philosopher, the big picture guy who could act as Trump's ideological conscience. "Tactical brilliance does not compensate for strategic incompetence," said a former Defense Department official who backs Trump. "The Trump administration was a rare administration to have a strategic thinker with wide knowledge of history [in Bannon]. It gave them a conceptual framework for the development of policies and counter policies. Our enemies are longer-term thinkers. They can target us with things like IEDs and be effective against us if we don't have a strategy. They don't care about sanctions and things like that. For the first time I saw, with Bannon and someone like Sebastian Gorka [a White House national security aide who left soon after Bannon did], highly intellectual officials who think, 'How do we defeat these terrorists?' It's now a war of ideas. There are very few people in the government who can think strategically and tactically. The people who existed back in World War II and launched our approach to communism were strategic thinkers. Now, there's no attention span."

★

When Trump and Bannon entered the White House, many of their critics, and much of the Left, exclaimed it was the beginning of a new "fascist" administration. But in Trump's first seven months in office, the period in which Bannon served, there was no danger of Trump acting like a fascist—indeed he had far more respect for the constitutional limits of presidential power than his predecessor and a great desire to shrink and not expand the power of the federal government. Even beyond that, it often seemed that the president faced not one but two opposition parties in Congress as he was stymied by the Republicans almost as much as the Democrats. There was no danger to constitutional checks and balances in the Trump administration. In fact, one could argue that Barack Obama, with his desire to expand the federal government, his determination to sidestep Congress with executive orders, such as the ones he issued on immigration, and his reinterpretation of laws already passed, such as the Clean Air Act, came much closer to the kind of fascism that Trump was supposedly going to inflict on the country.

Trump and Bannon wanted to move quickly on the administration's top priorities. Some actions, like slashing the federal regulatory burden, attracted relatively little attention. Others, like stemming the flow of illegal immigration and preventing terrorists from entering the country, became major sources of contention. On Friday, January 27, just a week after being inaugurated, Trump signed an executive order barring for ninety days the entry of people into the United States from seven countries, previously identified by the Obama administration as "countries of concern," where terrorists are prevalent and the government is either hostile to the United States or in a state of turmoil or unable to perform adequate background checks on travelers. These countries were Iraq, Iran, Libya, Somalia, Sudan, Syria, and Yemen. The order also refused entry to refugees from any country for 120 days and imposed an indefinite prohibition on the entry of Syrian refugees. The Trump administration wanted the ninety- to 120-day ban to give the Department of Homeland Security time to draw up new procedures for "extreme vetting" that would help keep foreign terrorists out of the United States.

An uproar ensued as refugees and immigrants were stopped at airports, and Democrats and Republicans both expressed exasperation at the hastiness with which the order was signed. Democrats and leftist protestors angrily termed the order a "Muslim ban." The courts blocked it and the White House eventually drew up a new one that did not include Iraq but continued to ban new entrants from Iran, Libya, Somalia, Sudan, Syria, and Yemen. The new order removed the indefinite ban on Syrian refugees and allowed people from any country who already held a valid visa to enter America. It continued to ban refugees for 120 days, except for those already "scheduled for transit" by the State Department. Much of the new order was upheld, at least temporarily, by the Supreme Court.

Bannon, with the whiteboard in his office and his eagerness to check off Trump campaign promises as accomplished, took the brunt of the blame for the administration moving too quickly. But he says the uproar had its upside: It helped create "the resistance" that Bannon believes thoroughly delegitimizes the Democratic Party with average voters it needs to win elections. He claimed he knew the outrage was coming, and that the Left had fallen into a trap. "The Left bit on it, and created the resistance, and it blew up, and now it's part of the political movement," Bannon said. "It's what's broken the Democratic Party," which has become a mere anti-Trump party that gives aid, comfort, and protection to sometimes violent street protestors. Even those who might be attracted to the policies of Bernie Sanders will be put off by the extremism they see among hardcore leftists, giving Republicans room to transform themselves into a party that appeals to workers. "It's also taken away Bernie's ability to actually reconstitute Democratic nationalism. You can't do it while the resistance is there; it won't allow it, *will not allow it, can't happen.* It's the greatest guarantor that we at least get some traction in building this worker's party."

Moreover, the focus on the travel ban kept the heat off a second order that Bannon says was much more significant, the "Border Security and Immigration Enforcement Improvements" order signed January 25. That measure called for building the wall with Mexico to keep out illegal immigrants and for hiring five thousand more border agents. It also put in place provisions to ease the removal of undocumented immigrants and end "catch and release," a practice that basically allowed captured illegal immigrants to go free on the mere promise that they would show up for their court date.

The order led to a dramatic change for the better in defending our national borders and upholding federal immigration law. "President Trump has directed his administration to enforce the nation's immigration laws more aggressively, unleashing the full force of the federal government to find, arrest and deport those in the country illegally, regardless of whether they have committed serious crimes," the *New York Times* bellowed the following month. "Documents released…by the Department of Homeland Security revealed the broad scope of the president's ambitions: to publicize crimes by undocumented immigrants; strip such immigrants of privacy protections; enlist local police officers as enforcers; erect new detention facilities; discourage asylum seekers; and, ultimately, speed up deportations."[4] Bannon thinks the order provides wide latitude to expel illegal immigrants. "If you read this, we think they actually have authority to deport all 11 million," he said.

Concluding that the United States was now serious about deporting them, illegal immigrants stopped showing up at the border. From February to June 2017, apprehensions at the border were down 58 percent compared to the same period a year earlier.[5] "A lot of the discussion about changes in our enforcement policy and the way we are going about doing business, we believe that has deterred people," said Homeland Security Department spokesman David Lapan. "When you get here, it is likely you are going to get caught. You are going to be returned to your country."[6]

Bannon says Trump's reduction of illegal immigration is already having a positive effect on the economy. "The thing with the restrictions on immigration is that we're finally stopping importing so much foreign labor here," he said. "So now you've got wages coming up. People have more discretionary money to spend."[7] But even with the reduction, Trump plans to fulfill his campaign promise to build the border wall with Mexico, no matter what, according to Bannon. Congress must appropriate the money to construct it, and it will have a fight on its hands if it doesn't. "He has reemphasized to me 100 times: *We must build the wall*," Bannon said. "The wall is going to take on totemic value. He is bound and determined. And by the way, if that takes shutting down the government, you know, he may have to do it.[8]

In early August 2017, Trump, with Bannon doing the legwork, went even further, touting legislation by Senators Tom Cotton and David Perdue that would scale back legal immigration and give preference to immigrants with employable skills.

Bannon believes immigration is an issue of historic importance—and that the failure of European leaders to control immigration from outside the continent could spell Europe's "doom." "They've got a massive problem," Bannon said in July 2017. "This migration problem from the south is *the* existential threat to Europe. It's everything. All the stories out in the last couple of days just about how Italy is not going to be able to handle it, and they're looking to the EU to bail them out, and the EU is basically saying, 'Hey, we've got to let more guys in.'"

Bannon continued, "It's not just their doom. What about us?" He expressed his frustration to a German official during a trip to

Europe. "What's most disturbing, is that you've let in anywhere from a million to a million-five Syrians," Bannon said. He told the official these refugees don't have reliable documents; it's impossible for the Europeans to tell who they are; and many of the "refugees" are young men who don't fit most people's image of a refugee. Europe is unmistakably importing some criminals and terrorists, and Bannon warned that these Syrian "refugees" will eventually be eligible for a visa waiver program to get into the United States. "If they get a German passport which—they're all going to get a German passport—the visa waiver program gets them into the United States," he said. "Just get on a plane and come here to the United States and you're here as a tourist or you're here as whatever. Principally, you've got what, sixty or seventy percent young men— how many combat divisions of potential terrorists do you think you've got in that? It's just this kind of not looking reality in the face."[9]

Bannon boasts about both the immigration and travel ban orders. "The deportation one has been an enormous success. The travel ban, or what has been called the travel ban, has been a success also," he said. "I believe it will be upheld in the courts, and it's given the Department of Homeland Security time to actually think through what extreme vetting is, so we got where we're actually going to have an organized process of how we vet people that come into this country."[10]

In an August 2, 2017, piece in *The Atlantic*, hardly a bastion of pro-Trump cheerleading, titled "Trump Has Quietly Accomplished More Than It Appears," author David Graham lists a string of Trump accomplishments largely ignored by the press. "There is so much attention paid to the chaos in the executive branch that it's easy to come to believe that Trump is getting nothing whatsoever accomplished," he writes. However, what Graham terms a "shadow government" is racking up significant achievements. "Even as the public government sputters, other elements of the Trump administration are quietly remaking the nation's regulatory landscape, especially on the environment and criminal justice." Graham dismisses that these accomplishments are part of a deliberate strategy on the part of the White House, because he believes the Trump administration is incapable of such sophistication. "But warnings that the Trump administration is doing X to distract from Y seem misguided for a couple of reasons—one being that they ascribe a greater organization that the White House evinces in any other sphere, and another being that the supposedly distracting stories are often just as catastrophic," he writes.[11]

But that's not completely correct. Bannon suggests extensive planning and strategizing occurred behind the scenes to try to advance all facets of the Trump agenda, and that the White House is driving reform within federal agencies and departments. Graham notes that Housing and Urban Development Secretary Ben Carson remarked to the *Washington Examiner*, "I'm glad that Trump is drawing all the fire so I can get stuff done."[12] Bannon thinks the Left is so distracted with its protests and its fear-mongering and its hatred of Trump that it is missing where Trump is quietly advancing his policies. "As long as they're involved in identity politics, as long as they think 'It's alt-right, and racism, and anti-Semitism,' they're never going to focus on what the real issues are, which is really about working class economics. That's all I'm focused on. And as long as they can't answer that...they're in a cul-de-sac that they literally can't get out of to win. And that's the place that I want them in right now."[13]

Bannon believes that Democrats' obsession with identity politics, while it stirs up a lot of noise on the fringes, is going to backfire even with some of the groups they're trying to inflame. He believes that African Americans, for instance, want better lives, not to be baited by race talk. "I come from a black working-class neighborhood," he said. "I know what they want—it was in the inaugural—they want safe streets for their families, good schools for their kids, and a great job for themselves. That's all they want," and the Trump administration is dedicated to providing just that.[14]

Also in the first few days of his presidency, Trump began taking historic action on trade, implementing his "America First" program. Bowing somewhat to the free traders within his administration, he agreed to renegotiate the North American Free Trade Agreement rather than simply withdraw from it. Bannon thinks the result may be an end to NAFTA anyway, though, because he believes the renegotiation will fail. But Trump was unequivocal about removing the United States from the Trans-Pacific Partnership, a vast trading alliance that included Canada, Mexico, Japan, Australia, New Zealand, Chile, Peru, Malaysia, Singapore, Vietnam, and Brunei, and which Trump believed undermined American sovereignty and economic (especially manufacturing) interests. The withdrawal from the Trans-Pacific Partnership was one of Trump's most significant moves, but because it was a complex issue and not something that it could vent about, the press paid it relatively little attention even though Trump's action was opposed by the entire Washington establishment—Democrats, establishment Republicans, and big business. While the press was obsessed with an unproven theory that the Trump campaign had "colluded" with the Russians (whatever that might mean) and with Trump's daily attack bait on his twitter feed, the president and his strategic advisor racked up other victories. America's NATO allies, in response to the president's America First agenda, committed to spending more on their own defense. Bureaucratic regulations on businesses, energy especially, were being removed at a rapid rate. The National

Association of Manufacturers (NAM) said Trump's deregulatory efforts had helped boost business confidence to a twenty-year high. "One of the biggest changes is the trajectory of regulatory burdens over the course of this presidency," said Rosario Palmieri, NAM vice president of labor, legal, and regulatory policy.[15]

★

On June 1, 2017, Bannon scored perhaps the greatest achievement of his short tenure in the White House. In a Rose Garden ceremony, Trump announced that the United States would not be party to the Paris climate change accords. Trump and Bannon viewed this as a vote in favor of American manufacturers and against foreign bureaucrats interfering with American sovereignty. In taking this action, Trump rejected the advice of his daughter Ivanka and son-in-law Jared Kushner and resisted pressure from globalists in the White House, including National Economic Council Director Gary Cohn.

Though the decision was Trump's, Bannon takes credit for laying the groundwork. "I'm very proud of [getting the United States out of] the Paris Accord, getting us out of all the environmental nonsense, all the environmental deals that were terrible for the country, that were there to suppress our economic growth and allow polluters like China to have free reign," Bannon told me. "Getting us out of TPP and the Paris accords—these international accords that restrict the United States from taking individual actions—I was very proud of blowing up all that stuff."[16]

One thing that Bannon and Trump did not want to blow up was the world. Contrary to the image sometimes painted of them as a pair of pugilists destined to get the United States into a catastrophic war, Bannon and Trump wanted to steer the United States clear from foreign interventions wherever possible. When Trump finally accepted his generals' recommendation to send more troops to Afghanistan, he did so reluctantly and only because he felt they had made an overwhelming argument that it was the best course of action he had, given the situation he had inherited from President Obama.[17]

"He's not trigger happy in wars," Bannon said. "He's amazingly reflective. When these options are given to him, he always wants the most reflective option that really limits the exposure of the United States militarily unless it's absolutely necessary. And then it's [his instinct] to go in whole hog."[18]

Bannon says people misunderstand the thinking behind Trump's America First ideology. It's not isolationism and it doesn't mean never intervening overseas, he says. "It's a false thing to say he's an isolationist. He's anything but an isolationist," Bannon said of Trump. "What he's not is a globalist. He's not going to let the power of the United States be dissipated out at these international organizations. No one has gone and engaged with the Islamic community as President Trump did in that speech" in Saudi Arabia in May 2017, where his audience included the leaders of more than fifty Muslim-majority nations, and he told them that they had to "take the lead in combating [Islamist] radicalization." Trump also said, "America is a sovereign nation and our first priority is always the safety and security of our citizens. We are not here to lecture— we are not here to tell other people how to live, what to do, who to be, or how to worship. Instead, we are here to offer partnership—based on shared interests and values—to pursue a better future for us all." That was Trump's foreign policy in a nutshell.[19]

What Trump seeks is a far more judicious use of American military power and a far greater emphasis on our allies pulling their weight to meet international challenges. During his May 2017 trip to Saudi Arabia, he signed a $110 billion arms deal with the Saudis, strengthening the Gulf state as a regional counterweight to Iran. In his speech, he inveighed against Islamist extremism and preached cooperation between America and the Gulf States. "The whole thing is, let the people in the region solve the problems. It's not America leading with troops or even money," Bannon said. "It is America understanding vital national security interests of the United States and having partners in regions where the vital national security interest of the United States dovetails with the interests of regional powers. And they get active and they take the lead and we're there."

This, Bannon said, contrasted with "the neocons and [George W.] Bush," who in his view overemphasized the leading role of the United States. The new approach, Bannon said, is analogous to Trump's business strategy of putting his brand on a building while others "provide the capital," the local knowledge, and "the manpower to get it done."

Implicit in the America First ideology, ironically enough, is a deeper respect for other cultures than was shown by the Obama administration and liberals and neocons, all of whom claim to be enlightened and educated but really think, wrongly, that the entire world wants to be progressive and liberal like they are, in Bannon's view. Bannon says, "I respectfully submit, democracy takes a while for people to be ready for. You can't force it. One of the things you're going to see with Trump is, whether it's in the Middle East, in the Gulf, or whether it's in Afghanistan, we are not going to enforce a Western solution on different cultures." While the Left chants that Trump is a fascist and a hater, he is, in fact, pursuing a foreign policy that holds other cultures in far higher respect. Bannon asserts that Trump puts a lot of emphasis on understanding foreign cultures in part because of his experience negotiating business deals overseas.

"That's why I think Trump is so perfect," Bannon says. Trump is "a New York City street guy" who is savvy and understands people from a wide variety of backgrounds and cultures. "He's dealt with a lot of characters," Bannon said. "I admire when he deals with these world leaders." He says people like Indian Prime Minister Modi, Egyptian President el-Sisi, and Chinese President Xi relate well to Trump because he treats them like equals. "It's not professorial Obama that you're going to get." Trump doesn't lecture other leaders; he listens. But when he thinks America is being threatened, as was the case with North Korea in the summer of 2017, he is quite content to be bold and assertive in defending America's interests.

While Trump and Bannon are reluctant interventionists, they also believe in a simple, Reaganite grand strategy that can be summed up in four words: "We win, they lose." President Trump means to eradicate the threat of Islamist terror, especially its presence as a presumed state or Caliphate under ISIS. "It's a total change in attitude and a real plan to actually win, of having victory," Bannon told me. "Mosul fell today—one-half of the physical Caliphate [of ISIS], is gone, within six months of Trump taking office. Raqaa will fall in a couple of weeks. And so his initial promise to eradicate the Caliphate of ISIS has begun. We've actually destroyed the physical caliphate. Obviously, ISIS is still a massive problem, but we've destroyed the physical caliphate."[20]

Some of this is a continuation of policies begun by Obama. But when he entered the White House, Trump ordered a review of our military strategy against ISIS and Islamist terror and demanded a more aggressive approach.

"First, he delegated authority to the right level to aggressively and in a timely manner move against enemy vulnerabilities," said Defense Secretary James Mattis on May 19, 2017. "Secondly, he directed a tactical shift from shoving ISIS out of safe locations in an attrition fight to surrounding the enemy in their strongholds so we can annihilate ISIS. The intent is to prevent the return home of escaped foreign fighters."

Bannon said destroying the "physical caliphate" was Mattis's chief goal since the start of the administration. "Jim Mattis's thing from day one was, we are not going to have a war of attrition, we are going to have a war of annihilation," Bannon said.

★

On July 6, 2017, President Trump delivered a rousing speech in Krasiński Square in Warsaw, Poland.

The president praised the Poles for their gallant attempt against all odds to combat the Nazis, and for their later proud resistance against Communist tyranny.

"Your oppressors tried to break you, but Poland could not be broken," Trump declared. "The memories of those who perished in the Warsaw Uprising cry out across the decades," he said. "Those heroes remind us that the West was saved with the blood of patriots; that each generation must rise up and play their part in its defense."

Trump said it was the same courage shown by the people of Poland, who cried out, during the Communist occupation, "We want God," that must save the West today. Against the advice of some of his senior aides, Trump said in his speech, "We are confronted by another oppressive ideology—one that seeks to export terrorism and extremism all around the globe. We are fighting hard against radical Islamic terrorism, and we will prevail. We cannot accept those who reject our values and who use hatred to justify violence against the innocent."

Trump, more optimistic than Bannon, said other Europeans, in addition to the Poles, also cry out for God. "Our citizens did not win freedom together, did not survive horrors together, did not face down evil together, only to lose our freedom to a lack of pride and confidence in our values," Trump said. "We did not and we will not. We will never back down. As long as we know our history, we will know how to build our future."

"The fundamental question of our time is whether the West has the will to survive," Trump said. "Do we have the confidence in our values to defend them at any cost? Do we have enough respect for our citizens to protect our borders? Do we have the desire and the courage to preserve our civilization in the face of those who would subvert and destroy it?"

Trump acknowledged that there was rot from within the West, a rot that stemmed not only from fading traditional values and religious faith, but from diminishing liberty, and a growing state. "The West became great not because of paperwork and regulations but because people were allowed to chase their dreams and pursue their destinies," Trump said. "Americans, Poles, and the nations of Europe value individual freedom and sovereignty. We must work together to confront forces, whether they come from inside or out, from the South or the East, that threaten over time to undermine these values and to erase the bonds of culture, faith, and tradition that make us who we are. If left unchecked, these forces will undermine our courage, sap our spirit, and weaken our will to defend ourselves and our societies."

Trump said, "I declare today for the world to hear that the West will never, ever be broken. Our values will prevail. Our people will thrive. And our civilization will triumph."

The Poles responded with a resounding acclamation: "Donald Trump! Donald Trump! Donald Trump!"[21]

Never since Ronald Reagan had any president stated the American cause, and the cause of Western civilization, better. It was also an address that echoed the philosophy that was at the core of Bannon, one Bannon had expressed most eloquently in his 2004 movie, *In the Face of Evil*, and in his 2014 speech to the Vatican. It was an ideology that was imbued in all six of his most cherished books, both the religious texts and the works by Gibbon, Thucydides, and Plutarch about classical Rome and Greece.

It was an ideology that represented Bannon's years of tireless reading, reflection, filmmaking, and journalism, and it was now being expressed to the world by the president of the United States, who shared Bannon's thinking. Trump said that the West stood for God, for the good, and for freedom, and that it was under attack, and that it must defend itself.

The Return of the Rebel

Bannon left the White House on August 18, 2017, the very day that President Trump ordered a formal investigation of China's theft of America's intellectual property, a first step in a possible major revamping of Sino-American trade policy—something that Bannon ardently supported against the globalists and free traders of the Washington establishment. The ongoing, but too often unrecognized, economic war with China was, Bannon believed, another great civilizational threat. "All we will be remembered for in a hundred years," Bannon told me after he left the White House, "is how we confronted China in the great economic war."

"Of the two most powerful countries in the world, one country in the next 25 or 30 or 40 years will become a global hegemon," he said. "Either us or them, and we are losing badly, and the elites in this town, the elites on Wall Street, do not want to—even the elites in Silicon Valley who need protection, or who are begging us for protection behind closed doors—don't want to confront it."[1]

Bannon immediately resumed command at Breitbart after he left the White House and he told me, "Half of what I do going forward is gonna be regarding China," because unfair Chinese trade practices were one of the greatest threats to the American System protecting the interests of the American worker and American manufacturing. "Everybody knows we're at economic war, and everybody knows we're losing," Bannon told me. He intended to reverse that—and he thought he had a better opportunity to fight that battle, and many others, outside the White House, unconstrained by the restrictions of practical politics.

The proximate cause of Bannon's exit from the White House is debated. There is little question that Bannon had grown weary of the place and that a part of him longed to leave and resume advancing the populist agenda from outside the West Wing. But the rebel had also long ago alienated various constituencies within the White House, including the tandem he derisively referred to as "Javanka," Jared Kushner and Ivanka Trump, and there were reports he was pressured to leave, at least earlier than he might have wished.

I met with him two days after his August 18 departure from the White House. He was ensconced in "the Breitbart Embassy," his Washington home, seated at the large dining room table where he had held countless meetings with a variety of aides, powerful backers, and leading conservative politicians and thinkers. Far from despondent, he was revved up and engaged, calling Breitbart staffers to bark out orders and planning the next phase of his life, which would have no less drama than any of the others as he prepared to continue advancing the principles for which he had always stood.

He had put himself on a severe new dietary regimen, deter-mined to lose weight and get in shape for the battles to come. Bags of Doritos had already been banished to the trash. Before him rested a mug containing a mysterious thick green concoction, as yet untouched, no doubt comprised of some combination of ingre-dients designed to ruthlessly attack and remove fat cells. Somebody drifted into the room to serve him a small ceramic cup containing a vinegary solution which he reluctantly downed, screwing up his face as he did. This might not be so easy. But he was determined.

Before him lay a vast political campaign—against the radical Islamists; against the mercantilist Chinese; against the Left and Antifa; against the globalists on Wall Street, Silicon Valley, and the Washington establishment; against the craven Republican accom-modationists who feared the liberal media and were weak and ineffective allies for Trump. Against them all, he was ready to fight to the end—a rebel to the last.

Acknowledgments

I am most grateful to my editor, Harry Crocker, for his excellent work, and to his fellow Regnery editor, Tom Spence, for thinking of me to do this book. I am also thankful to my project editor, Nancy Feuerborn, for the fine job she did, to Regnery President Marji Ross for agreeing to allow an author who had not yet published a major book to write for her company, and to all the others at Regnery who worked on this project.

I am very thankful to my wife, Rebekah Koffler, and to my children, Adam and Ariela, for their patience with me as I wrote this, sometimes crankily, and for pretty much going without me during the summer of 2017. I am also thankful to my mother, Dr. Sandra Koffler, and my siblings, Lauren O'Neill and Jonathan Koffler, for their love and support. And finally, I thank my late father, Dr. David Koffler, for his love and for teaching me from an early age the principles of conservative thought.

Notes

Introduction

1. Interview with the author, July 30, 2017.

Prologue

1. Remarks of President Donald J. Trump—As Prepared for Delivery, Inaugural Address, January 20, 2017, https://www.whitehouse.gov/inaugural-address.

Chapter 1

1. Interview with the author, July 13, 2017.
2. Interview with the author, July 30, 2017.
3. Interview with the author, July 30, 2017.
4. Interview with the author, July 13, 2017.
5. Interview with the author, July 30, 2017.
6. Interview with the author, July 28, 2017.
7. Interview with the author, July 30, 2017.

8. Interview with the author, July 30, 2017.

9. Interview with the author, August 4, 2017.

10. Matea Gold, Rosalind S. Helderman, Gregory S. Schneider, and Frances Stead Sellers, "For Trump Advisor Stephen Bannon, Fiery Populism Followed Life in Elite Circles," *The Washington Post*, Nov. 19, 2016, https://www.washingtonpost.com/politics/for-trump-adviser-stephen-bannon-fiery-populism-followed-life-in-elite-circles/2016/11/19/de91ef40-ac57-11e6-977a-1030f822fc35_story.html?utm_term=.b52866340f71.

11. Interview with the author, August 4, 2017.

Chapter 2

1. Graham Moomaw, "Steve Bannon Talks Richmond Roots, Says Trump Will Condemn All Forms of Racism," *Richmond Times-Dispatch*, Nov. 26, 2017, http://www.richmond.com/news/local/government-politics/steve-bannon-talks-richmond-roots-says-trump-will-condemn-all/article_0f87d838-4aaa-5e4f-b717-6a342a00b89c.html.

2. Interview with the author.

3. Ibid.

4. Robby North, "Trump top adviser Bannon got his political start in Blacksburg," The Roanoke Times, Nov. 17, 2016, http://www.roanoke.com/news/education/higher_education/virginia_tech/trump-top-adviser-bannon-got-his-political-start-in-blacksburg/article_ac3c9d68-3e1e-5926-b13d-2ad02bad3915.html.

5. Ibid.

6. Interview with author, July 21, 2017.

7. Interview with the author, July 14, 2017.

8. Ibid.

9. Interview with the author, July 17, 2017.

10. "History of Women at Virginia Tech," accessed Aug. 14, 2017, http://www.wlp.givingto.vt.edu/history/.

11. Interview with the author, July 30, 2017.

12. Interview with the author, July 14, 2017.

13. Interview with the author, July 21, 2017.

14. Interview with the author, July 14, 2017.

15. Interview with the author, July 14, 2017.

16. Interviews with the author, July 30, 2017.

17. Matea Gold et al, "For Trump Adviser Stephen Bannon, Fiery Populism Followed Life in Elite Circles," *The Washington Post*, Nov. 19, 2016, https://www.washingtonpost.com/politics/for-trump-adviser-stephen-bannon-fiery-populism-followed-life-in-elite-circles/2016/11/19/de91ef40-ac57-11e6-977a-1030f822fc35_story.html?utm_term=.8536acd5d31d.

18. Ibid.

19. Ibid.

20. Interview with the author, July 17, 2017.

21. Interview with the author, July 14, 2017.

22. Interview with the author, July 21, 2017.

23. Interview with the author, July 17, 2017.

24. Interviews with the author, July 30, 2017.

Chapter 3

1. https://assets.documentcloud.org/documents/3438272/Bannon-OMPF.pdf.

2. Michael Kranish and Craig Whitlock, "How Bannon's Navy Service During the Iran Hostage Crisis Shaped His Views," *The Washington Post*, Feb. 10, 2017, https://www.washingtonpost.com/politics/how-bannons-navy-service-during-the-iran-hostage-crisis-shaped-his-views/2017/02/09/99f1e58a-e991-11e6-bf6f-301b6b443624_story.html?utm_term=.1c7e40d42d66.

3. Douglas Kennedy, "The making of Steve Bannon, from Young Navy Man to White House Power Player," Fox News, March 30, 2017, http://www.foxnews.com/politics/2017/03/30/fox-news-exclusive-making-steve-bannon-from-young-navy-man-to-white-house-power-player.html.

4. Interview with the author, July 18, 2017.

5. Ibid.

6. Michael Kranish and Craig Whitlock, "How Bannon's Navy Service During the Iran Hostage Crisis Shaped His Views," *The Washington Post*, February 10, 2017, https://www.washingtonpost.com/politics/how-bannons-navy-service-during-the-iran-hostage-crisis-shaped-his-views/2017/02/09/99f1e58a-e991-11e6-bf6f-301b6b443624_story.html?utm_term=.1c7e40d42d66.

7. Interview with the author, July 13, 2017.

8. Interview with the author, July 18, 2017.

9. Robert C. Roth, "Armed Forces Snapping To for President," *Los Angeles Times*, Feb. 27, 1981, http://latimesblogs.latimes.com/thedailymirror/2011/02/military-snaps-to-attention-for-reagan.html.

10. Naval History and Heritage Command, U.S. ship force levels, https://www.history.navy.mil/research/histories/ship-histories/us-ship-force-levels.html.

11. Ronald Reagan, "Remarks on Presenting the Medal of Honor to Master Sergeant Roy P. Benavidez," Feb. 24, 1981, http://www.presidency.ucsb.edu/ws/?pid=43454.

12. Interview with the author, July 21, 2017.

13. Interview with the author, July 18, 2017.

14. Ibid.

15. Mark D. Faram, "Steve Bannon and the National Security Council: What We Can Learn from His Navy Career," *Navy Times*, Feb. 1, 2017, http://www.navytimes.com/news/your-navy/2017/02/01/steve-bannon-and-the-national-security-council-what-we-can-learn-from-his-navy-career/.

Chapter 4

1. Matt Viser, "Harvard Classmates Barely Recognize the Bannon of Today," *The Boston Globe*, November 26, 2017, https://www.bostonglobe.com/news/politics/2016/11/26/look-steven-bannon-and-his-years-harvard-business-school/B2m0j85jh5jRKzKbMastzK/story.html.

2. Duff McDonald, "How Harvard Business School Helped Turn Steve Bannon into a Monster," *Vanity Fair*, April 19, 2017, https://www.vanityfair.com/news/2017/04/steve-bannon-harvard-business-school.

3. Interview with the author, July 28, 2017.

4. Ibid.

5. Joshua Green, "This Man Is the Most Dangerous Political Operative in America," *Bloomberg Businessweek*, October 8, 2015, https://www.bloomberg.com/politics/graphics/2015-steve-bannon/.

6. Michael Kranish and Craig Whitlock, "Stephen K. Bannon, Architect of Anti-globalist Policies, Got Rich as a Global Capitalist," *The Washington Post*, March 31, 2017, https://www.washingtonpost.com/politics/stephen-k-bannon-architect-of-antiglobalist-policies-got-rich-as-a-global-capitalist/2017/03/31/47382082-0a8b-11e7-a15f-a58d4a988474_story.html?utm_term=.3f9525594f49.

7. Interview with the author, July 28, 2017.

8. Ibid.

9. Bill Dietrich, "Biosphere—Learning from Failure," *The Seattle Times*, November 8, 1994.

10. Victoria Loe, "While New World," Dallas Morning News, November 13, 1995.

11. "Stephen Bannon Talkes Biosphere 2," https://www.youtube.com/watch?v=l_gkBPlLcfQ.

12. Eric Stern, "Manager vowed revenge on Ailing, her lawyer says," *Tucson Citizen*, May 24, 1996.

13. Rex Weiner, "Left Coast Dealmaking Savvy," *Variety*, November 17–23, 1997.

14. Interview with the author, August 4, 2017.

15. Interview with the author, July 30, 2017.

16. Interview with the author, August 4, 2017.

17. Scott Hettrick and Susanne Aunt, "Genius Has a Library Card," Daily Variety, March 22, 2005.

18. Shawn Boburg and Emily Rauhala, "Stephen Bannon Once Guided a Global Firm That Made Millions Helping Gamers Cheat," *The Washington Post*, August 4, 2017.

19. Interview with the author, July 30, 2017.

20. Matea Gold et al, "For Trump Adviser Stephen Bannon, Fiery Populism Followed Life in Elite Circles," *The Washington Post*, November 19, 2016, https://www.washingtonpost.com/politics/for-trump-adviser-stephen-bannon-fiery-populism-followed-life-in-elite-circles/2016/11/19/de91ef40-ac57-11e6-977a-1030f822fc35_story.html?utm_term=.1956ef86d9a2.

Chapter 5

1. Asawin Suebsaeng, "I Watched All of Steve Bannon's Bad Movies," *Daily Beast*, August 19, 2016, http://www.thedailybeast.com/i-watched-all-of-steve-bannons-bad-movies.

2. Adam Wren, "What I Learned Binge-Watching Steve Bannon's Documentaries," *Politico*, December 2, 2016, http://www.politico.com/magazine/story/2016/12/steve-bannon-films-movies-documentaries-trump-hollywood-214495.

3. "Political Vindication Radio: The Stephen K. Bannon Interview," https://www.youtube.com/watch?v=Ng3gktU2vpw&t=1732s.

4. James Ulmer, "On the Right Side of the Theater Aisle," *New York Times*, June 26, 2005, http://www.nytimes.com/2005/06/26/movies/on-the-right-side-of-the-theater-aisle.html?_r=0.

5. Interview with the author, July 9, 2017.

6. Bannon Interview with Political Vindication Radio, Fall 2010.

7. Interview with the author, July 9, 2017.

Chapter 6

1. Interview with the author, July 9, 2017.

2. Ibid.

3. *Generation Zero*, directed by Stephen Bannon, Citizens United Productions, 2010. Interview with the author, July 9, 2017.

4.   Ronald Reagan, "Encroaching Control," March 30, 1961, https://
     www.youtube.com/watch?v=SDouNtnR_IA.
5.   *Generation Zero*, directed by Stephen Bannon, Citizens United
     Productions, 2010.
6.   Philip Ewing, "Fact Check: Has President Obama 'Depleted' the
     Military?" NPR, April 29, 2016, http://www.npr.
     org/2016/04/29/476048024/fact-check-has-president-obama-
     depleted-the-military.
7.   2017 Annual Report of the Boards of Trustees of the Federal
     Hospital Insurance and Federal Supplementary Medical Insurance
     Trust Funds, https://www.cms.gov/Research-Statistics-Data-and-
     Systems/Statistics-Trends-and-Reports/ReportsTrustFunds/
     Downloads/TR2017.pdf.
8.   Address to the Liberty Restoration Foundation, October 25, 2011.
9.   "End of an Era for Goldman," CNN, May 3, 1999, http://money.
     cnn.com/1999/05/03/markets/goldman/.
10. Interview with the author, July 9, 2017.
11. Ibid.

Chapter 7

1.   Hadas Gold and John Bresnahan, "Trump Campaign CEO Once
     Charged in Domestic Violence Case," *Politico*, August 25, 2016,
     http://www.politico.com/story/2016/08/steve-bannon-domestic-
     violence-case-police-report-227432.
2.   Ibid.
3.   Elizabeth Chuck et al., "Trump Campaign CEO Steve Bannon
     Accused of Anti-Semitic Remarks by Ex-Wife," NBC News, August
     27, 2016, http://www.nbcnews.com/politics/2016-election/trump-
     campaign-ceo-steve-bannon-accused-anti-semitic-remarks-
     ex-n638731.
4.   Tracy Nelson, "Set Up for Success," Army West Point, October 3,
     2009, http://goarmywestpoint.com/news/2009/10/3/Set_Up_For_
     Success.aspx.

5. Graham Moomaw, "Steve Bannon Talks Richmond Roots, Says Trump Will Condemn All Forms of Racism," *Richmond Times-Dispatch*, November 26, 2016.

6. Gold and Bresnahan, "Bannon Accused of Anti-Semitic Remarks."

7. Jessica Lipscomb, "As Steve Bannon Rose to Power, His Ex-Wife Struggled with Drugs and Violence in Miami," *Miami New Times*, January 27, 2017, http://www.miaminewtimes.com/news/as-steve-bannon-rose-to-power-his-ex-wife-struggled-with-drugs-and-violence-in-miami-9096063.

8. Ben Shapiro, "I Know Trump's New Campaign Chairman, Steve Bannon. Here's What You Need to Know," *The Daily Wire*, November 13, 2016.

9. Hadas Gold, "Steve Bannon's 'Tough Love,'" *Politico*, September 2, 2016, http://www.politico.com/story/2016/09/steve-bannon-breitbart-employees-criticize-227672.

10. Andrew Blake, "Kurt Bardella, Former Breitbart Spokesman, Blasts New Trump Campaign Chief Bannon as 'Dictator,'" *The Washington Times*, August 20, 2016, http://www.washingtontimes.com/news/2016/aug/20/kurt-bardella-former-breitbart-spokesman-blasts-ne/.

11. Gold, "Steve Bannon's 'Tough Love.'"

12. Ibid.

13. Interview with the author, July 30, 2017.

14. James Delingpole, "It's Tough Being the Only British Journalist Who's Right about Everything," *The Spectator*, November 19, 2016, https://www.spectator.co.uk/2016/11/its-tough-being-the-only-british-journalist-whos-right-about-everything/.

Chapter 8

1. Interview with the author, July 30, 2017.

2. Interview with the author, July 28, 2017.

3. Ross Fuller, *The Brotherhood of the Common Life and Its Influence* (New York: State University of New York Press, 1995), 89.

4. Ibid., 108.

5. Ibid., 109, 144.

6. Ibid., 157.

7. Thomas à Kempis, *The Imitation of Christ*, chapter 30, http://biblehub.com/library/kempis/the_imitation_of_christ/the_thirtieth_chapter_the_quest.htm.

8. Ignatius of Loyola, *The Spiritual Exercises of St. Ignatius of Loyola*, https://www.ccel.org/ccel/ignatius/exercises.ix.html.

9. Ibid., "Particular and Daily Examen," https://www.ccel.org/ccel/ignatius/exercises.xii.ii.html?highlight=one,ought,to,propose,guard,himself,with,diligence,against#highlight.

10. Interview with the author, July 30, 2017.

Chapter 9

1. Interview with the author, July 30, 2017.

2. Interview with the author, July 9, 2017.

3. J. Lester Feder, "This Is How Steve Bannon Sees the Entire World," BuzzFeed News, originally posted on November 15, 2016, updated on November 16, 2016, https://www.buzzfeed.com/lesterfeder/this-is-how-steve-bannon-sees-the-entire-world?utm_term=.otb9WdZL2#.km62l35bX.

4. Christopher Lasch, *The Revolt of the Elites and the Betrayal of Democracy* (New York: W. W. Norton & Company, 1996), 28, 39, and 41.

5. Ibid., 27.

6. Interview with the author, July 9, 2017.

7. Ibid.

8. Ibid.

9. J. Lester Feder, "This Is How Steve Bannon Sees the Entire World," BuzzFeed News, originally posted on November 15, 2016, updated on November 16, 2016, https://www.buzzfeed.com/lesterfeder/this-is-how-steve-bannon-sees-the-entire-world?utm_term=.otb9WdZL2#.km62l35bX.

10. Interview with the author, July 30, 2017.

11. Bannon on Political Vindication Radio, July 5, 2011.

12. Michael Lind, *Land of Promise: An Economic History of the United States*, (New York: Harper, 2012), 145.

13. Interview with the author, July 9, 2017.

14. William J. Gill, *Trade Wars against America*, (Westport, CT: Praeger, 1990), xii.

15. Michael Lind, *Land of Promise: An Economic History of the United States*, (New York: Harper, 2012), 143.

16. Interview with the author, July 9, 2017.

17. Ibid.

18. Interview with the author, July 9, 2017.

19. Ibid.

20. Interview with Donald Trump, Breitbart News Daily, November 5, 2015, https://soundcloud.com/breitbart/breitbart-news-daily-donald-trump-november-5-2015.

21. Interview with the author, July 30, 2017.

22. Ibid.

Chapter 10

1. J. Lester Feder, "This Is How Steve Bannon Sees the Entire World," BuzzFeed News, originally posted on November 15, 2016, updated on November 16, 2016, https://www.buzzfeed.com/lesterfeder/this-is-how-steve-bannon-sees-the-entire-world?utm_term=.otb9WdZL2#.km62l35bX.

2. Interview with the author, July 9, 2017.

3. Abdel Fattah el-Sisi in a speech; Dana Ford, Salma Abdelaziz, and Ian Lee, "Egypt's President Calls for a 'Religious Revolution,'" CNN, updated January 6, 2015.

4. Ibid.

5. Feder, "How Bannon Sees the World."

6. Interview with the author, July 9, 2017.

7. Ibid.

8. Interview with the author, July 30, 2017.

9. Ibid.

10. Feder, "How Bannon Sees the World."
11. Interview with the author, July 30, 2017.
12. Ibid.

Chapter 11

1. Interview with Sean Hannity, "Exclusive Look at 'Generation Zero,'" Fox News, February 23, 2010, www.foxnews.com/story/2010/02/24/exclusive-look-at-generation-zero.html.
2. Interview with Political Vindication Radio, Fall, 2010.
3. "Fire from the Heartland Discussion with Director Steve Bannon: The Rise of Tea Party Women," YouTube video, 11:04, posted by "Melissa Clouthier," September 20, 2010, https://www.youtube.com/watch?v=LcGGUwDDz0A.
4. Interview with Political Vindication Radio, Fall, 2010.
5. "Fire from the Heartland Discussion with Director Steve Bannon: The Rise of Tea Party Women," YouTube video, 11:04, posted by "Melissa Clouthier," September 20, 2010, https://www.youtube.com/watch?v=LcGGUwDDz0A.

Chapter 12

1. Interview with the author, July 9, 2017.
2. Hannity interview with Bannon about The Undefeated, "Inside New Sarah Palin Documentary Hitting Theaters This Summer," Fox News Shows, June 10, 2011, http://www.foxnews.com/transcript/2011/06/10/inside-new-sarah-palin-documentary-hitting-theaters-this-summer.htm.
3. Bannon on the Rusty Humphries Show, July 15, 2011.
4. Hannity interview with Bannon about The Undefeated, "Inside New Sarah Palin Documentary Hitting Theaters This Summer," Fox News Shows, June 10, 2011, http://www.foxnews.com/transcript/2011/06/10/inside-new-sarah-palin-documentary-hitting-theaters-this-summer.htm.
5. Ibid.
6. Bannon on Political Vindication Radio, July 5, 2011.

7.   Interview with the author, July 9, 2017.

Chapter 13

1.   Joshuah Green, "This Man Is the Most Dangerous Political Operative in America," *Bloomberg Businessweek*, October 8, 2015, https://www.bloomberg.com/politics/graphics/2015-steve-bannon/.

2.   Matea Gold, "The Mercers and Stephen Bannon: How a populist power base was funded and built," *The Washington Post*, March 17, 2017.

3.   R. Kinsey Lowe, Conservative Filmmakers Get a Fest of Their Own," *Lost Angeles Times*, September 30, 2004, http://articles.latimes.com/2004/sep/30/news/wk-lowe30.

4.   Interview with the author.

5.   Rebecca Mead, "Rage Machine," *The New Yorker*, May 24, 2010, http://www.newyorker.com/magazine/2010/05/24/rage-machine.

6.   Stephen K. Bannon, "Breitbart in the World," Breitbart, March 1, 2013, http://www.breitbart.com/big-journalism/2013/03/01/breitbart-in-the-world/.

7.   Interview with the author, July 30, 2017.

8.   Ibid.

9.   Ibid.

10.   Sarah Posner, "How Donald Trump's New Campaign Chief Created an Online Haven for White Nationalists," *Mother Jones*, August 22, 2016, http://www.motherjones.com/politics/2016/08/stephen-bannon-donald-trump-alt-right-breitbart-news/.

11.   Interview with the author, July 30, 2017.

12.   Matea Gold et al., "For Trump Adviser Stephen Bannon, Fiery Populism Followed Life in Elite Circles," *The Washington Post*, November 19, 2016, https://www.washingtonpost.com/politics/for-trump-adviser-stephen-bannon-fiery-populism-followed-life-in-elite-circles/2016/11/19/de91ef40-ac57-11e6-977a-1030f822fc35_story.html?utm_term=.5e1e0fc4c2bc.

13.   Matt Viser, "Harvard Classmates Barely Recognize the Bannon of Today," *Boston Globe*, November 26, 2016, https://www.bostonglobe.

com/news/politics/2016/11/26/look-steven-bannon-and-his-years-harvard-business-school/B2m0j85jh5jRKzKbMastzK/story.html.

14. Paul Bond, "Steve Bannon's Former Hollywood Partner Breaks Silence: 'He's Not a Racist' (Q&A)," *The Hollywood Reporter*, May 8, 2017, http://www.hollywoodreporter.com/news/steve-bannons-hollywood-partner-breaks-silence-defends-hes-not-a-racist-q-a-1001006.

15. Interview with the author, July 30, 2017.

16. Becket Adams, "The Lewandowski-Fields Incident: A Complete Timeline," *Washington Examiner*, March 30, 2016, http://www.washingtonexaminer.com/the-lewandowski-fields-incident-a-complete-timeline/article/2587171.

17. Joel B. Pollak, "The Scrum: Video Shows Lewandowski Reaching in Michelle Fields's Direction," Breitbart, March 11, 2016, http://www.breitbart.com/big-government/2016/03/11/trump-presser-ben-terris-misidentified/.

18. Rosie Gray and McKay Coppins, "Michelle Fields, Ben Shapiro Resign from Breitbart," *BuzzFeed News*, originally posted on March 14, 2016, updated on March 14, 2016, https://www.buzzfeed.com/rosiegray/michelle-fields-ben-shapiro-resign-from-breitbart?utm_term=.ukgN9E6OV#.lqzRpOqKa.

19. Lloyd Grove, "Breitbart Rolls Over after Reporter 'Grabbed' by Trump Aide," *Daily Beast*, March 9, 2016, http://www.thedailybeast.com/breitbart-rolls-over-after-reporter-grabbed-by-trump-aide?platform=hootsuite.

20. Ibid.

21. Matthew Boyle, "Text Messages: Lewandowski Never 'Acknowledged' Grabbing Michelle Fields, Despite Erroneous Daily Beast Report," Breitbart, March 11, 2016 http://www.breitbart.com/big-government/2016/03/11/text-messages-lewandowski-never-acknowledged-grabbing-michelle-fields-despite-erroneous-daily-beast-report/.

22. Interview with the author, July 30, 2017.

Chapter 14

1.   Frank Clifford, "Non-Candidate Trump Talks Tough on Political Issues," *Los Angeles Times*, October 23, 1987, http://articles.latimes.com/1987-10-23/news/mn-10766_1_speech.

2.   Colin Campbell, "'I think I'd Win': Donald Trump Teased a Presidential Run to Oprah in 1988," *Business Insider*, September 11, 2015, www.businessinsider.com/donald-trump-to-oprah-in-1988-win-president-2015-9.

3.   Interview with the author, July 9, 2017.

4.   "Bannon's War," PBS Frontline documentary.

5.   Conversation with the author, July 30, 2017.

6.   Eliana Johnson and Eli Stokols, "What Steve Bannon Wants You to Read," *Politico*, February 7, 2017, www.politico.com/magazine/story/2017/02/steve-bannon-books-reading-list-214745.

7.   Hillary Clinton, "Transcript: Hillary Clinton's DNC Speech, Annotated," by *Los Angeles Times* staff, *Los Angeles Times*, July 28, 2016, www.latimes.com/politics/la-na-pol-hillary-clinton-convention-speech-transcript-20160728-snap-htmlstory.html.

8.   Sean Trende, "The Case of the Missing White Voters, Revisited," RealClearPolitics, June 21, 2013, https://www.realclearpolitics.com/articles/2013/06/21/the_case_of_the_missing_white_voters_revisited_118893.html.

9.   Interview with the author, July 9, 2017.

10. Kellyanne Conway, Poll on Immigration, http://caffeinatedthoughts.com/wp-content/uploads/2014/08/08-19-14-Woman-Trend-Poll.pdf.

11. Molly Ball, "The Unsung Architect of Trumpism," *The Atlantic*, March 20, 2017, https://www.theatlantic.com/politics/archive/2017/03/kellyanne-conway-trumpism/520095/.

12. Ross Douthat, "How Trump Might Win," *New York Times*, September 14, 2016, https://www.nytimes.com/2016/09/14/opinion/campaign-stops/how-trump-might-win.html.

13. Interview with the author, July 9, 2017.

14. Ken Stern, "Exclusive: Stephen Bannon, Trump's New C.E.O., Hints at His Master Plan," *Vanity Fair*, August 17, 2016.

15. Interview with the author.

Chapter 15

1.   Ryan Lizza, "How Climate Change Saved Steve Bannon's Job," *The New Yorker*, June 2, 2017.

2.   Interview with the author, July 9, 2017.

3.   Ibid.

4.   Michael D. Shear and Ron Nixon, "New Trump Deportation Rules Allow Far More Expulsions," *New York Times*, February 21, 2017, https://www.nytimes.com/2017/02/21/us/politics/dhs-immigration-trump.html.

5.   D'Angelo Gore and Eugene Kiely, "Trump's Border Boast," FactCheck.org, July 31, 2017, http://www.factcheck.org/2017/07/trumps-border-boast/.

6.   Stephen Dinan and Andrea Noble, "Trump's Immigration Enforcement Helps Slow Illegal Border Crossings by 76%," *The Washington Times*, May 9, 2017, http://m.washingtontimes.com/news/2017/may/9/illegal-immigration-southwest-border-down-70-pct/.

7.   Interview with the author, August 20, 2017.

8.   Interview with the author, July 9, 2017.

9.   Ibid.

10. Interview with the author, August 20, 2017

11. David A. Graham, "Trump Has Quietly Accomplished More Than It Appears," *The Atlantic*, August 2, 2017, https://www.theatlantic.com/politics/archive/2017/08/what-trump-is-actually-accomplishing/535458/.

12. Sarah Westwood and Al Weaver, "Ben Carson's Quiet Life in a Chaotic Cabinet," *Washington Examiner*, July 21, 2017, http://www.washingtonexaminer.com/ben-carsons-quiet-life-in-a-chaotic-cabinet/article/2629281.

13. Interview with the author, July 9, 2017.

14. Interview with the author, July 30, 2017.

15. S. A. Miller, "Donald Trump's Deregulation Boosts Manufacturing Confidence," *The Washington Times*, June 15, 2017.

16. Interview with the author, August 20, 2017.

17. Susan B. Glasser, "The Trump White House's War Within," *Politico Magazine*, July 24, 2017, http://www.politico.com/magazine/story/2017/07/24/donald-trump-afghanistan-215412.

18. Interview with the author July 9, 2017.

19. Transcript of Trump's Speech in Saudi Arabia, updated May 21, 2017, http://www.cnn.com/2017/05/21/politics/trump-saudi-speech-transcript/index.html.

20. Interview with the author, July 9, 2017.

21. Remarks by President Trump to the People of Poland, July 6, 2017, https://www.whitehouse.gov/the-press-office/2017/07/06/remarks-president-trump-people-poland-july-6-2017.

Epilogue

1. Interview with the author, August 20, 2017.

Index

A

Access Hollywood, 162
Affinity Media Holdings, 44
African Americans, 14, 140, 176
à Kempis, Thomas, 2, 79
Alberice, Peter, 20, 22–23, 25, 32, 45
Aldrin, Buzz, 60
Alinsky, Saul, 62, 130
American Film Renaissance, 48
Antifa, 130, 187
Antifragile, 157
Arlington Cemetery, 26
AT&T, 11, 83–84
Atlantic, The, 174
Augustine, Margret, 41–42

B

Baby Boomers, 58–61, 63–64, 66–67
Bachmann, Michele, 120–21
Bannon, Chris, 10, 14–18, 39, 42–44, 71
Bannon, Martin, Sr., 10–13, 28, 65
Bannon, Martin "Mike," III, 10–11, 15, 17, 21–22, 24
Bannon, Mary Beth, 2, 10, 13, 16, 23, 25, 43, 92, 142
Bannon, Maureen, 20, 69–70, 75
Bannon, Sharon, 9–10, 12–13, 25
Bannon, Stephen,
    and family, 9–18, 69–82
    and filmmaking, 47–68
    and politics, 83–132, 147–184
    at Breitbart, 133–146
    in school, 19–26, 35–46
    in the Navy, 27–34
Bannon & Co., 38–39, 42, 75
Bardella, Kurt, 72
Barnes, Fred, 123
Bass, Edward, 41
Battle for America, 118, 123
Benavidez, Roy, 31
Benedictine High School, 17, 19, 24, 28, 76–77
Best and the Brightest, The, 111
Bethlehem Steel, 14
Biosphere 2, 40–42
Bossie, David, 57–58, 60, 147, 154
Breitbart, Andrew, 119, 128, 130, 136–37, 140
Breitbart News, 3, 43, 71–74, 97, 99, 115, 118–19, 134, 136–40, 142–45, 152, 186
Brotherhood of the Common Life and Its Influence, The, 2, 77
Bryan, William Jennings, 154
Brzezinski, Mika, 164
Burton, Dan, 57
Bush, Billy, 162
Bush, George W., 67, 168, 179
Bush, Jeb, 155, 163

C

Carson, Ben, 175
Carter, Jimmy, 29–32
Castle Rock Entertainment, 40
Catholic Church, the, 74, 78, 84
Chesapeake and Potomac Telephone
    Company (C&P), The, 11
Chicago Mercantile Exchange, 117
Christie, Chris, 153
Churchill, Winston, 50, 163
Civil War, 64, 93, 129, 163
Clay, Henry, 93–95
Clinton, Bill, 57, 135–36, 110, 153,
    155, 169
Clinton, Hillary, 6, 57–58, 62, 87, 90,
    134–36, 141–42, 149, 152–54,
    155–58, 161
Clinton Cash (book), 134–35
Clinton Cash (movie), 135
Clinton Foundation, 135–36
Clisham, Gary, 24
Clohesy, Diane, 69, 71
Cloward, Richard, 61–62
CNBC, 117
Coburn, Tom, 123
Cohn, Gary, 168, 177
Cold War, 49
Columbia University, 41, 62
Conservative Political Action Confer-
    ence (CPAC), 126
Conway, Kellyanne, 160–61
Coolidge, Calvin, 38
Corbyn, Jeremy, 90
Costa, Robert, 153
Cotton, Tom, 173
Coulter, Ann, 120–23
Cruz, Ted, 155
Cupp, S. E., 120

D

Daily Beast, the, 47, 144
Darby, Brandon, 73
DeBerry, Marshall, 24
Delingpole, James, 73–74, 131
Democratic Party, 30, 32, 111, 135,
    152, 171
Democrats, 5–6, 9, 23, 30, 32, 58, 90,
    93, 110–11, 117, 123, 126–27, 129,
    131, 134–37, 142, 146, 152, 156,
    158–60, 168, 170–71, 175–76
Department of Homeland Security,
    170, 172, 174
Dobbs, Lou, 123
Douthat, Ross, 161–62
Duck Dynasty, 108

E

el-Sisi, Abdel Fattah, 105–6, 180
Evola, Julius, 113–15
Extortion: How Politicians Extract
    Your Money, Buy Votes, and Line
    Their Own Pockets, 134

F

Fields, Michelle, 72, 142–45
Fire from the Heartland, 48, 118–21,
    123, 125
First Turning, 59–60
Fourth Turning, 63–64, 67–68, 163–
    64
Fourth Turning, The, 58, 162
Fox News, 58, 118, 144
Fuller, Ross, 2, 77

G

Gansfort, Wessel, 78

Generation Zero, 60–61, 63, 65, 67, 91, 130
Genius Products, 44
Georgetown University, 15, 33
Gibbon, Edward, 2, 100, 112, 183
Gibson, Mel, 48
Gill, William J., 94
Gingrich, Newt, 123
Ginter Park, 10, 43
Ginter Park Community Center, 14
Giuliani, Rudolph, 130
Glamour, 21
Goldman Sachs, 36–37, 44–45, 51, 65–67, 73, 76, 89, 127, 148
Goldman Sachs: The Bank That Runs the World, 66
Government Accountability Institute (GAI), 133–36
Graham, David, 174–75
Grant, Ulysses S., 163
Groote, Gerard, 78–79, 115
Guénon, René, 114–15

H

Halberstam, David, 111–12
Hambros, 75–76
Hamilton, Alexander, 92–95
Hannity, Sean, 58, 65, 67, 118
Hanson, Victor Davis, 60
Harvard Business School, 12, 33, 35–37, 71, 77, 99, 127, 141
Herr, Doris Virginia Anita, 11–12, 14
Hillary: The Movie, 58
History of the Decline and Fall of the Roman Empire, The, 2, 100
History of the Peloponnesian War, The, 2, 111
Ho Chi Minh, 24

Hollywood, 13, 37, 48–49, 89, 124, 141, 146, 148
Hoover, Herbert, 93
Hope and the Change, The, 129–30
Horowitz, David, 130, 142
Houff, Cathleen "Susie," 20, 69
House Oversight Committee, 57
Howe, Neil, 59–60, 62, 64, 67
Hubbell, Webster, 58

I

IGE (Internet Gaming Entertainment), 44
Ignatius of Loyola, 2, 77, 79–80, 115
IMI Exchange, 44
Imitation of Christ, The, 2, 79, 115
In the Face of Evil: Reagan's War in Word and Deed, 45, 48–49, 136, 141, 183
Islam, 3, 29, 49–54, 103–7, 109, 114, 142, 178–81, 187

J

James, Nat, 14
Jarrett, Valerie, 168
Jeopardy!, 2
Jones, Julia, 140

K

Kaplan, Rob, 37
Kasich, John, 155
Kelly, John, 165
Kennedy, John F., 12–13, 24, 32, 155
Khomeini, Ruhollah, 104
King, Martin Luther, Jr., 109
Kirkpatrick, Jeane, 32
Krivoruchka, Mark, 20

Kushner, Jared, 153, 155, 165, 177, 186

Kwatinetz, Jeff, 141

L

Lapan, David, 173
Lasch, Christopher, 87–89
Leary, Timothy, 60
Lee, Thai, 141
Lewandowski, Corey, 72, 142–45
Liberty Film Festival, 48, 136
Lincoln, Abraham, 93–95, 163
Lind, Michael, 93
Lindsey, Bruce, 169
Lives of the Noble Greeks and Romans, 2, 112
Loesch, Dana, 120–21
London, England, 75–77, 89, 100, 105, 107
Lord of the Rings, The, 48
Los Angeles, CA, (LA), 37, 75, 77

M

Malkin, Michelle, 120
Man and His Becoming According to the Vedanta, 115
Marlow, Alex, 72
Masso, Sonny, 28–33
Mattis, James, 180–81
McCain, John, 58, 126, 128, 161
McGovern, George, 23
McLaughlin, Mike, 20, 24
McSweeney, Pat, 10, 12, 14, 17, 30
Mercer, Rebekah, 133, 137
Mercer, Robert, 133, 137
Milken, Michael, 37
Miller, Stephen, 7–8, 153
Modi, Narendra, 90, 180

Morning Joe, 164
Morris, Dick, 123
Morris, Philip, 25
MSNBC, 164
Mussolini, Benito, 50, 63, 113

N

National Association of Manufacturers (NAM), 176–77
Navy, the, 13, 22, 25, 27–28, 30–33, 35–36, 48, 73, 76, 80, 115
Nazis, Nazism, 49–50, 108–9, 113, 181
Nevin, Darrell, 21, 25
New York City, NY, 37, 51, 76, 89, 130, 146–47, 180
New Yorker, The, 166
New York Times, 48, 113, 136, 161, 172
Norfolk, VA, 9, 11
North American Free Trade Agreement (NAFTA), 176
Novak, Michael, 61
Novak, Robert, 32

O

Obama, Barack, 5, 62–64, 105, 117–19, 121, 123–24, 129–31, 158, 168, 170, 178–80
Occupy Unmasked, 130-31
Officer Candidate School, 26
Oliver, Susan, 21–25
Oprah Winfrey Show, The, 148
Oracle, AZ, 40

P

Palin, Sarah, 125–29, 131, 149
Party of Davos, 89–91, 110, 146

Passion of the Christ, The, 48
Paulson, Hank, 67
Peña Nieto, Enrique, 155
Pentagon, the, 28, 31
Perdue, David, 173
Piccard, Mary Louise, 69–70, 142
Piven, Frances Fox, 61–62
Plutarch, 2, 112, 183
Politico, 47, 70
Pollak, Joel, 140, 143
PolyGram, 42
Preate, Alexandra, 70
Pulitzer, Joseph, 138
Putin, Vladimir, 113

R

Rachmaninoff, Sergei, 52
Rand, Ayn, 95
Reagan, Ronald, 30–32, 45, 48–49,
    51–53, 55, 57, 61, 127, 129, 136,
    141, 155–56, 162, 180, 183
Reagan's War, 42
RealClearPolitics, 159
Redford, Robert, 20
Republican National Committee
    (RNC), 151, 153
Republican National Convention, 129,
    139
Republican Party, 30, 97, 120–21, 129,
    142, 151–52
Republicans, 90, 92, 97, 117, 119, 124,
    126, 128, 131, 133-34, 137–38,
    145, 148, 151–52, 154, 161–62,
    168, 170–71, 176
*Revolt of the Elites and the Betrayal of
    Democracy, The*, 87
Rhodes Scholarship, 22
Richmond, VA, 9–12, 16–17, 25, 43,
    164

Riefenstahl, Leni, 49, 136
Riehl, Dan, 73
Robertson, Phil, 108–9
Rolling Stones, the, 164
Romney, Mitt, 131, 152, 159, 161
Roosevelt, Theodore, 85, 93, 95
Rove, Karl, 168
Rubio, Marco, 155, 163
Rules for Radicals, 62
Russia, Russians, 51, 110–11, 113–14,
    135, 141, 176

S

Saint Gertrude High School, 17
Sanders, Bernie, 90, 140, 171
Santelli, Rick, 117, 120
Scarborough, Joe, 164
Schlafly, Phyllis, 120, 122, 162
Schweizer, Peter, 45, 51–52, 65, 133–
    35, 141
Seagram Company, 42
Second Turning, 60, 64
Seinfeld, 40, 73
Sessions, Jeff, 7, 153
Shapiro, Ben, 72, 140, 143–45
Silicon Valley, 101, 146, 186–87
Société Générale, 42, 75–76
Solov, Larry, 140, 143
Song of Roland, The, 103
Spectator, The, 73
Spicer, Sean, 153, 168
*Spiritual Exercises of St. Ignatius of
    Loyola, The*, 2, 79, 115
Stepien, Bill, 153
Strauss, William, 59–60, 62, 64
Suebsaeng, Asawin, 47
Sullivan, George, 29

T

Taleb, Nassim Nicholas, 156–58
Tea Party, 69, 89, 117–21, 123, 125–
    26, 128–29, 131, 137, 145, 147, 162
Terris, Ben, 143–44
Third Turning, 62, 64, 67
Throw Them All Out, 134
Thucydides, 2, 111–12, 183
Tilney, Cornelia, 36
Time, 60
Toastmasters, 15
Torchbearer, 108
Trende, Sean, 159–60
Trump, Donald, 1, 3, 5–8, 39, 41, 68,
    72, 74, 87, 89–90, 93, 99, 111, 131,
    135, 142–83, 185–87
Trump, Ivanka, 177, 186
Turner, Ted, 40

U

Uber, 12
Undefeated, The, 126–27
United States of America, 1, 5, 27, 51,
    53, 61, 65, 92–94, 97–99, 107, 109,
    134, 137–38, 148, 156, 163, 165,
    170, 172, 174, 176–79, 183
University of Arizona, 42
USS *Paul F. Foster*, 27, 29

V

Vietnam War, 23–24, 30, 32
Virginia Tech, 18-21, 23–24, 45, 76
Vorse, Scot, 12, 36-40, 42, 71–72, 77

W

Wall Street, 13, 43, 66, 83, 85, 95, 101,
    130, 134, 159, 185, 187
Wall Street Journal, the, 33

Walsh, Katie, 153
Washington, D.C., 5–7, 31, 43, 48, 71,
    83, 89, 91, 105, 124–26, 128, 134,
    146, 149–50, 153, 160, 166–67,
    176, 185–87
Washington, George, 92, 94–5
Washington Examiner, the, 175
Washington Post, The, 44, 140, 143–
    44, 153
Weinberg, John, Jr., 37
Weinstein, Harvey, 44
Weinstein Company, The, 44
Western civilization, 2, 23, 32, 47,
    50–51, 86, 137, 184
Westinghouse Electric Corporation,
    39–40
White House, the, 1, 13, 16, 39, 43,
    126, 145, 152, 158, 165–66, 168–
    69, 171, 175, 177, 180, 185–86
Wolfson, Howard, 156
Woodstock, 60, 66
World War I, 50
World War II, 25, 59, 64–65, 68,
    92–93, 107, 111, 163, 169
Wren, Adam, 47, 136

X

Xi Jinping, 180

Y

Yiannopoulos, Milo, 139

Z

Zen Catholicism, 80